# The Laces of Ipswich

## THE ART AND ECONOMICS OF
## AN EARLY AMERICAN INDUSTRY,
## 1750–1840

*Marta Cotterell Raffel*

University Press of New England

HANOVER AND LONDON

UNIVERSITY PRESS OF NEW ENGLAND

37 LAFAYETTE STREET, LEBANON, NH 03766

© 2003 BY UNIVERSITY PRESS OF NEW ENGLAND

PRINTED IN THE UNITED STATES OF AMERICA

5 4 3 2 1

This book was published with the support of the Great Lakes Lace Group, Inc.

CIP data appear at the end of the book

# Contents

# Acknowledgments

The work of this research and the writing of this book have been a journey into the eighteenth century. Along the way many people and institutions provided their insights, time, and encouragement and have allowed me to examine and learn from the treasures in their holding. I will never forget the great opportunity I have had in working with and learning from these individuals.

The Smithsonian Institution has done an exceptional job in preserving its artifacts and contributing to this research. Kathy Dirks of the National Museum of American History has provided expert fiber analysis. Her love of history and keen scientific eye have been invaluable. Doris Bowman graciously provided the lace artifacts in the collection for study. Karen Thompson and Sheryl DeJong have generously cared for the lace collection. The insights of these talented lace makers have been very helpful. Paul Peterson of the National Museum of Natural History, Washington, D.C., gave of his time to examine the Ipswich bobbins.

Gerard W. Gawalt of the Library of Congress, Washington, D.C., and the remarkable staff there tirelessly provided opportunities for me to study the laces and documents. They have done an exceptional job of preserving and conserving these artifacts. Sylvia Albro and the paper conservation office have contributed expert fiber analysis and taught me the finer points of understanding parchment, fibers, and eighteenth-century paper. The enormous holdings of the library itself was a valuable resource. Bruce Martin in the reading room was of immense help when I was pressed by deadlines or needed help in locating a rare text.

Beth Gilgun taught me about eighteenth-century everyday clothing. Nancy Rexford allowed me access to her extensive library on early American clothing and generously shared her time so that I could study the Ipswich artifacts in the collection of the Danvers Historical Society, in Danvers, Massachusetts.

The Museum of Fine Arts, Boston, and Lauren Whitley are appreci-

ated for their time and efforts and allowing me to study the Ipswich artifacts in their collection.

The Old Newburyport Historical Society, Newburyport, Massachusetts, has been very helpful in giving me access to their eighteenth-century
account books and garments.

The Society for the Preservation of New England Antiquities in Cambridge, Massachusetts, including Jane C. Nylander, Melinda Linderer,
Lorna Condon, and their historical collection, library, and archives, has
been an appreciated resource.

Many organizations have provided assistance: the Baker Library at
Harvard University; the Connecticut Historical Society in Hartford,
Connecticut; the Hamilton Historical Society in Hamilton, Massa-
chusetts; the Holbrook Research Institute, Oxford, Massachusetts; the
Lexington Historical Society; the Massachusetts State Archives; the Na-
tional Archives, Washington, D.C.; the New England Historical Society;
the New England Historic Genealogical Society in Boston; the Rowley
Historical Society in Rowley, Massachusetts; the Topsfield Historical
Society in Topsfield, Massachusetts; the Valentine Museum in Richmond,
Virginia; the Wenham Historical Association and Museum, Inc., of
Wenham, Massachusetts; Beverly Johnson and the Wethersfield Histori-
cal Society, Wethersfield, Connecticut, which owns the portrait of Sarah
Noyes Chester; the Yale University Art Gallery, New Haven, Connecti-
cut, which owns the portrait of Mrs. Beardsley; and the Pennsylvania
Academy of the Fine Arts, Philadelphia, owns the portrait of Mrs. Con-
stant Storrs.

The Peabody Essex Museum and library in Salem, Massachusetts, has
been a tremendous resource for both its treasures of artifacts and its documents of early New England. Paula Richter's talents, dedication, and
expertise are greatly appreciated. Jane E. Ward was very helpful with the
archival records, account books, and original manuscripts.

Diane L. Fagan Affleck, Karen Herbaugh, Michael J. Smith, and all the
fine staff members of the American Textile History Museum in Lowell,
Massachusetts, have been supportive of this project from its beginning,
as has been George Washington's Mount Vernon, Estate and Gardens,
which owns Martha Washington's shawl.

A special note of appreciation is due to James Kyprianos, past curator,
Mary P. Conley, the late Dan Lunt Jr., Stephanie R. Gaskins, Elizabeth
Redmond, and all the fine members of the Ipswich Historical Society.
Over the years of doing research this charming community, the Histori-
cal Society, the City Hall, and the Ipswich Public Library became second

homes. I am very grateful for all the help, gracious welcomes, good wishes, remembrances, and enthusiasm.

In the field of historians two people really made this work possible. One is Richard M. Candee, Professor of American and New England Studies, Boston University, whose insight, knowledge, and delightful sense of humor were invaluable. The other is Laurel Thatcher Ulrich. Laurel is most noted for her wonderful books, *A Midwife's Tale* and *Goodwifes*. For me she is an unfailing guide to doing research well and understanding eighteenth-century living. Laurel's unpretentious and genuine nature only adds to her remarkable talents. Her direct and critical eye has been equally valuable and educational. I thank her for her time, insights, questions, and most of all for what she has taught all of us about everyday living in the seventeenth and eighteenth centuries.

It took more than historians and curators to accomplish this work. It took a lot of lace makers. I have learned something from each and every lace maker I have ever met. The conclusions in this book are my own and not necessarily the opinions of the persons listed here. However, what I have learned, I have learned from these talented people, and they are richly deserving of credit for the knowledge, skill, and time they have so generously devoted to the study of this industry.

The Great Lakes Lace Group supported this research and the publication of this book through a generous grant. This group is dedicated to studying and documenting all aspects of lace and lace history. To Trena Ruffner and every member of this group I give my heartfelt thank you. The Chesapeake Region Lace Guild is where this all began. Tamara Webb is both a dear friend and my first bobbin lace teacher. The other members of this fine guild have offered their interest, ideas, questions, and insights. Carol Watson has done some fine work on the Ipswich lace samples at the Library of Congress and has done an excellent analysis of the groundwork techniques. Jean Hoadley has helped me understand groundwork techniques, hosted meetings at her home, and made some of the most beautiful bobbins I have ever seen. Diana Lillevig offered her notable library, insights, and knowledge of box #4 of Alexander Hamilton's papers for the benefit of this research. Mary Lou Kueker, Armistice Turtora, and the good wishes of so many others are greatly appreciated.

The support of other lace makers has been especially meaningful. The New England Lace Guild and the International Old Lacers, Inc., has been particularly supportive. Susie Johnson worked with Carol Watson and did a very fine analysis of the samples of lace at the Library of Congress. Susie has a critical eye for detail and is dedicated to the scholarly research of the Ipswich laces, as is Laura Bensley. Holly Van Sciver is one of the finest lace teachers I've had the joy to meet. Her insights on Bucks lace, especially as it relates to the Ipswich laces, have been most valuable. Karen Thompson, Sheryl DeJong, Lia Baumeister, Christa Van Schagen, and Agnes V. Breemen have made notable contributions by taking on the time-consuming work of reproducing the Ipswich laces. To Doris May, I am very grateful for her insight and encouragement. Sally Barry has significantly contributed to the conservation and preservation of the Ipswich lace industry artifacts at the Ipswich Historical Society. Robin Lewis-Wild, another outstanding lace teacher, has contributed hours of her time and insight. Robin's knowledge and dedication to lace making is impressive. Her contributions to this work are beyond measure.

A note of gratitude goes to the Auclair family and also to the family of the late Stephen Paine. Mr. Paine was a fine gentleman, dedicated to preserving and understanding the wealth of artifacts in our museum collections.

One of the earliest voices of encouragement came from Jo Bidner. Jo's knowledge, guidance, and resourcefulness got this research under way. I am grateful to Pat Earnshaw for her thoughts and writings.

A day with Pam Nottingham taught me much about English lace and the strength of English tea. Her delightful spirit and exceptional knowledge provided a basis for understanding the type of lace made in Ipswich.

A very special thank you goes to Santina Levey, who has taken the time to answer so many questions. Santina is a true lace scholar. Her research is accurate, thorough, and insightful.

My most heartfelt thanks is due for the gentle support and understanding of my friends and family. Miriam and Bob Hawking provided a place to stay while in Massachusetts, helped me get last-minute slides duplicated for presentations, make catalogs, title slides, and hand out materials for lectures. Their friendship is one of the true joys of living. Haley, my dear little daughter, survived a life-threatening case of chicken pox just as I was discovering all the children lost in eighteenth-century New England to smallpox. Haley in her own little way has been supportive of this work only because she knows it is important to me. And for her that is enough. I am forever grateful for her life. And my gratitude to Gary Raffel for his devotion, understanding, and patience, which made the writing of this book possible.

M.C.R.

*The Laces of Ipswich*

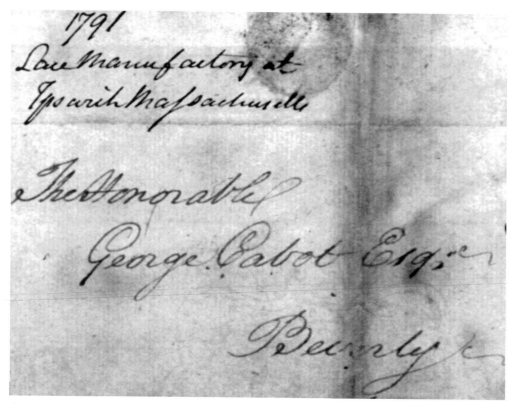

*Fig. 1.* "Lace Manufactory at Ipswich Massachusetts," reads the envelope addressed to George Cabot by Joseph Dana, who is reporting on the manufacturing of lace at Ipswich in 1791. *Courtesy of the Library of Congress, Washington, D.C.*

*The Making of an American Industry*

$\mathcal{T}$HIS IS THE STORY of a little-known American industry, the hand-made lace industry of Ipswich, Massachusetts. It is an introduction to a pivotal period of our history, based on the surviving artifacts and documents from the Ipswich lace industry, and it speaks to many interests: history, the development of industry, the lace itself, the work of women, and the life and times of early Americans. The chapter on the lace itself provides an additional and very detailed accounting for those who have a passion for the intricacies of lace and textiles, whereas the other chapters delve into the historical, social, and economic issues related to this industry and to the people who made or wore the lace.

Unfortunately, much of what we'd like to know about this industry is lost in the past, either because very few of the details of this industry were ever recorded or because most of the documents and objects related to the industry have long been lost. This book seeks to answer as many questions as possible on the basis of evidence contained in the remaining tools, samples of lace, record books, and other related items. But there are many questions about this industry that the artifacts and remaining records can't answer; and while it is very tempting to speculate, the better path is simply to present as much factual information as possible. Fortunately, the surviving objects and records are packed with data that tell a fascinating story of early American ingenuity.

*Almost Forgotten*

The industry of lace making in Ipswich, Massachusetts, is one of the most interesting endeavors of early New England, producing an article equally valued for its luxury and beauty, as well as its political, social, and economic significance. This industry, which began around 1750 and ended in the early 1840s, reveals an intriguing view into late-eighteenth-century and early-nineteenth-century American life. While the lace is of significance in terms of textile and lace history, the industry itself provides an invaluable look at various aspects of early American life that are rarely documented: changes in commerce and the move to a market economy; the development of trade from a system of barter to more sophisticated methods of bookkeeping and enterprise; the evolution of business strategies that began with the norms of domestic production and developed into a system of factories; the shift from the English pound to the American dollar; the everyday lives of women, their work, and their education; the changing social fabric of the day and its impact on the exchange of goods and services; and the significance of textiles in early American life.

In addition to these concerns, the Ipswich lace industry was a quiet witness to the American Revolution and the building of the American democratic system. The famous names, dates, and battles are well known; however, the routine of daily life as experienced by most people who lived during this period rarely finds its way into print.[1] The story of Ipswich lace provides us with a more personal understanding of the Revolution as it was observed by the common person and went unrecorded in famous books. These individuals simply worked to survive. For them the Declaration of Independence equated to a wrenching separation from their homeland, one that tore at the fabric of their politics, communities, belief systems, families, and the very sense of themselves as a community and a nation.

Over two hundred years later, Ipswich lace has stepped out of the anonymity of curious objects and dusty, long forgotten account books to take its place in American history and in the history of lace. The making of this lace transcends lovely adornment or the idyllic picture of the lace maker at a sunny doorway. Ipswich lace depicts the story of economic decline, social revolution, politics, and war. Significantly, Ipswich lace tells the history of ordinary people in an extraordinary time. Their contribution to this history memorializes an admirable spirit and the will to survive during times of dramatic change.

*A New Chapter in Lace History*

The handmade lace industry of Ipswich adds a new chapter to the history of lace, that of American Lace. Conventional thought suggested that commercial lace making confined itself to Europe and did not exist in the colonies. Existing documents and artifacts prove that Ipswich indeed existed as a commercial lace-making center on American soil.

In the eighteenth century, lace making was quite common. Not surprisingly, people immigrating to America from English and European lace-making regions brought their skills with them. When such individuals arrived in Ipswich, they initiated the events that led to the founding of the lace-making industry.

At present, Ipswich is the only area in the United States known to have successfully produced handmade bobbin lace on a sustained commercial level. Keeping proper young ladies and those without other means of support respectably employed by making lace was a popular goal. Scattered attempts to form lace-making industries—for instance, the nineteenth-century lace schools in Newport, Rhode Island, and Newburyport, Massachusetts[2]; efforts involving Native American groups; and the twentieth-century enterprise known as the Torchon Lace Company, which marketed the Princess Lace Machine—never seemed to reach beyond the dynamic personalities of their founders.

By contrast the Ipswich industry demonstrated a volume of production, a longevity (continuing through many generations), and a range of distribution that exceeded any other documented effort.

This first book on the history of commercial handmade lace in Ipswich, Massachusetts, pays homage to the women who developed this new lace and to those individuals who transported their skills, talents, and creativity to America.

*The Dana Letters and Lace Samples*

Research began at the Whipple House, in Ipswich, Massachusetts, built in 1655 and operated by the Ipswich Historical Society. Over many years and curators this seventeenth-century house acquired the largest array of Ipswich lace and lace-related tools.

Artifacts related to the industry are not limited to Ipswich. They can be found at least as far north as Newburyport, Massachusetts, and as far south as Richmond, Virginia. The Library of Congress houses one of the most important and rarest set of documents related to the Ipswich lace industry. These documents contain a report on the Ipswich lace manufactory and samples of Ipswich lace. These samples of Ipswich lace and related letters (fig. 2) have survived in the archival papers of Alexander Hamilton to provide a detailed record of the industry.[3]

Artifacts such as these 211-year-old lace samples (fig. 3) and accompanying letters are extremely rare for other reasons than their age. Some of

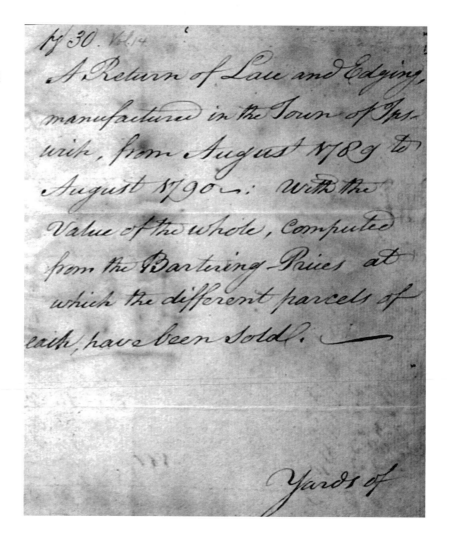

the laces were made of black silk, which predisposed them to the ravages of time. Comparing the strength and pliability of new silk with old silk demonstrates that exposure to light and the elements over time leaves the threads friable and brittle, which eventually results in disintegration of fibers. Additionally, the black dyes of this period are notorious for being very corrosive, often causing catastrophic damage. It is remarkable that the laces still exist after so much time and handling.

These lace samples and documents[4] have had an adventurous journey in their many years. They originated with Reverend Joseph Dana of Ipswich, Massachusetts, who collected the samples of lace between 1789 and 1790 when preparing his report to George Cabot. Mr. Cabot, a new senator, eagerly sent the parcel on to Tench Coxe, the assistant secretary of

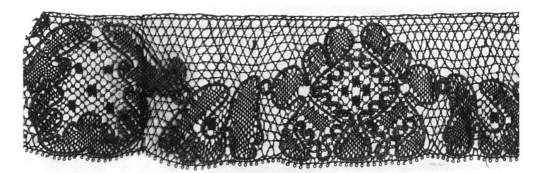

*Fig. 3.* Ipswich lace, black silk, ca. 1789–1790. *Courtesy of the Library of Congress, Washington, D.C.*

the treasury. Mr. Coxe received the "intelligence" with great enthusiasm. If American manufacturing had had a cheerleader, his name would have been Tench Coxe. His outspoken enthusiasm declared a spirit of "whatever you can do, we can do better" that gained him a reputation as a militant advocate of American manufacturing. With this treasured report and lace samples he went off to Philadelphia to give a lecture and show others what Ipswich had done. After his speech the package containing Joseph Dana's letter, thirty-six samples of lace, and enclosures was presented to Alexander Hamilton, secretary of the treasury. Hamilton then delivered a speech to Congress on December 5, 1791, in which he referred to the fine accomplishments of lace making in Ipswich. Joseph Dana's letter respectfully requests that when "the Honorable Body" is finished examining the samples of lace that they "be presented to the Beloved President of the United States and his Consort."[5] The State Department eventually came into possession of the report and lace samples as part of Alexander Hamilton's papers. Apparently, Mr. Hamilton never passed them on and chose instead to keep them in his own records. In 1848 the papers of Mr. Hamilton were purchased by the Library of Congress. Within these archival papers the report and laces from Ipswich arrived at the library, where they have been ever since and are now expertly preserved for further study.

*A Total of 41,979 Yards of Lace*

On January 24, 1791, Joseph Dana wrote his letter, with its enclosures, to provide for Mr. Cabot a clear understanding of the volume of lace produced annually and its market value. The fine script of the Rev. Mr.

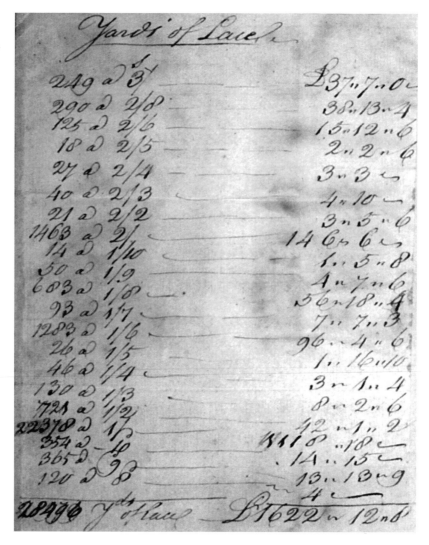

*Fig. 4.* Joseph Dana's listing of the amounts and prices of the wider laces sold between 1789 and 1790. *Courtesy of the Library of Congress, Washington, D.C.*

Dana's educated hand records that between August 1789 and August 1790 (see fig. 2) over six hundred women in Ipswich produced and sold 41,979 yards of bobbin lace (figs. 4 and 5). Production at such a level indicates more than a genteel pastime. In our mechanized world, yard goods (that is, goods produced and sold by the yard) are made by the tens of thousands. Turning thread into such an intricate fabric as handmade lace requires both skill and long hours of work. It is has been forgotten today that an average of seven inches of lace made per day, every day, by every lace maker[6] was a *large* quantity of lace, indicative of a very serious commitment to the industry.

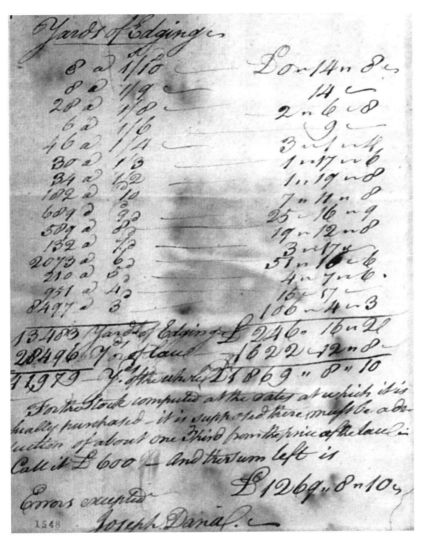

*Fig. 5.* A total of 41,979 yards of lace sold at the "Bartering price," a listing by the Rev. Mr. Dana of the amount of edgings sold and calculates the total amount of lace sold between 1789 and 1790 and its value before dealers markup. *Courtesy of the Library of Congress, Washington, D.C.*

*The First Census of the United States of America*

Joseph Dana's report, in conjunction with the first U.S. census (1790) under the newly ratified Constitution and the presidency of George Washington, answered vital questions. The number and types of industries were as important as the number of residents in each town. As this new government developed and became more sophisticated, it aggressively sought information on vital goods and services. The development and maintenance of industries within the United States competed with foreign trade, easing the need for imports. A multitude of trade, commerce,

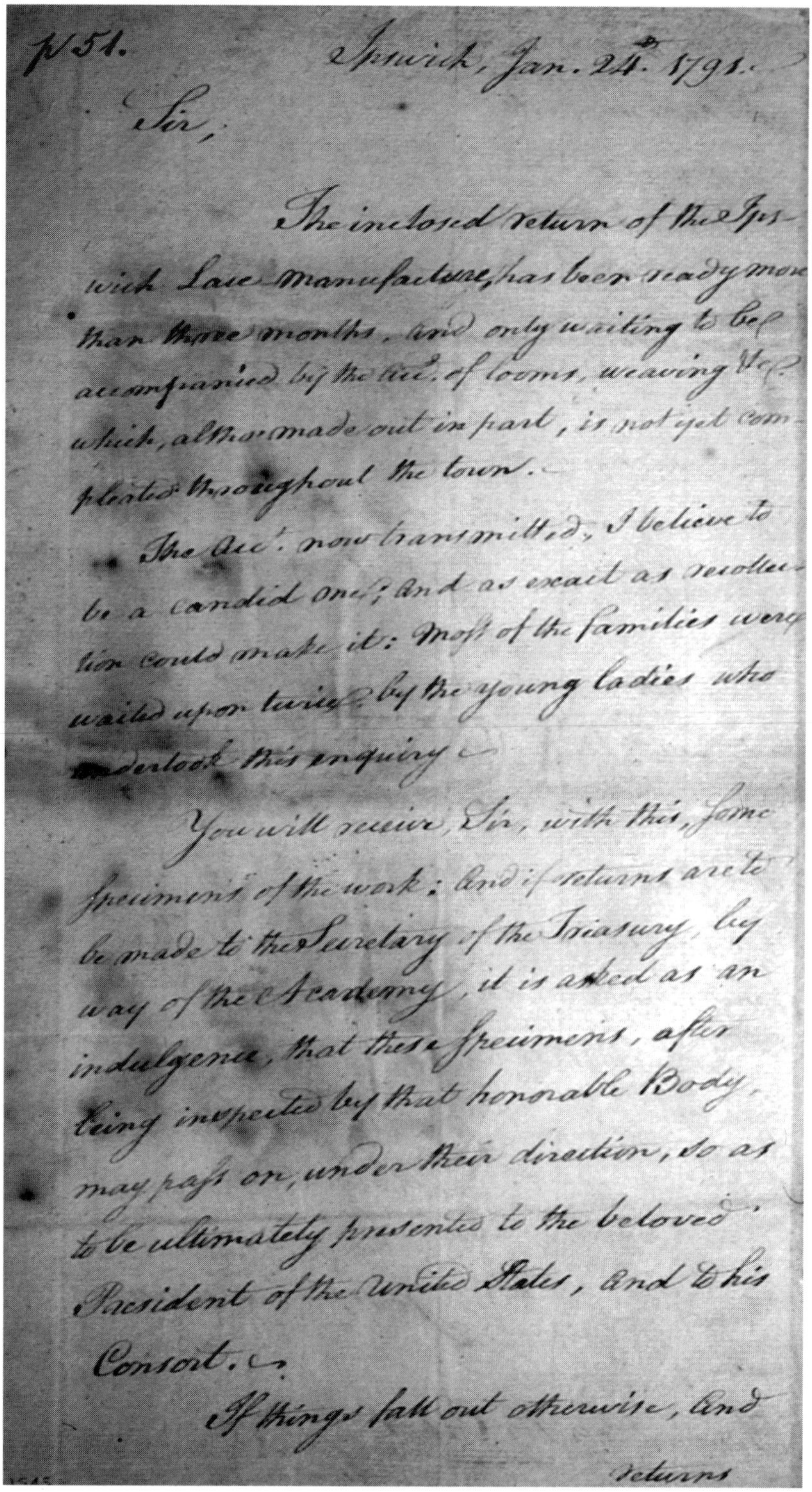

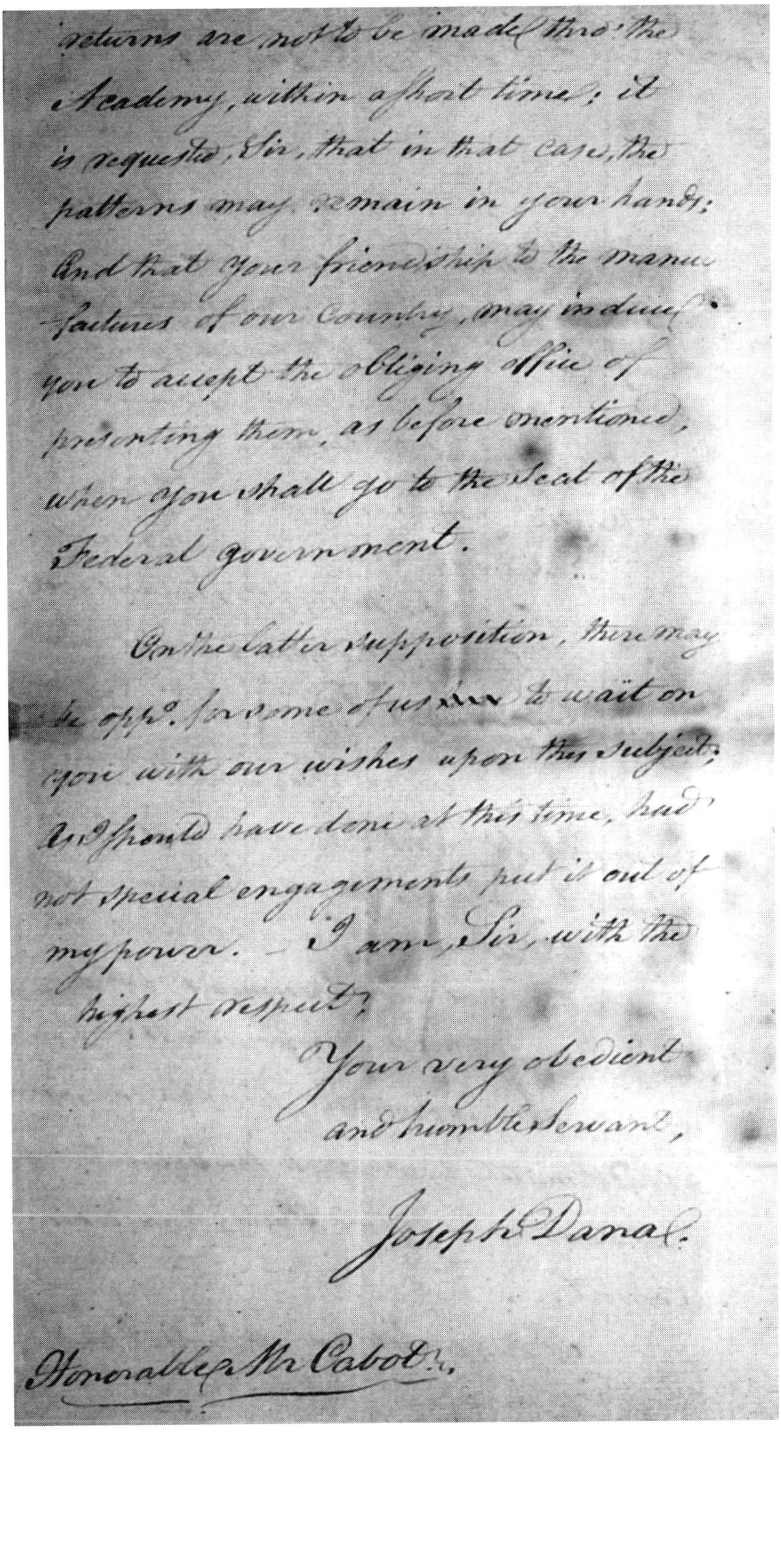

returns are not to be made thro' the
Academy, within a short time; it
is requested, Sir, that in that case, the
patterns may remain in your hands;
And that your friendship to the manufactures of our Country, may induce
you to accept the obliging office of
presenting them, as before mentioned,
when you shall go to the Seat of the
Federal government.

On the latter supposition, there may
be oppⁿ. for some of us now to wait on
you with our wishes upon this subject;
As I should have done at this time, had
not special engagements put it out of
my power. — I am, Sir, with the
highest respect,
Your very obedient
and humble Servant,

Joseph Dana.

Honorable Mr. Cabot.

*Fig.* 7. "I am, Sir, with
the highest respect . . .
Your very obedient and
humble Servant, Joseph
Dana," second page of
Joseph Dana's letter
dated January 24, 1791.
*Courtesy of the Library of
Congress, Washington, D.C.*

and taxing issues became the catalyst for many heated debates and ultimately legislation. Newspapers of the day discussed these issues at length, defining even the smallest details, such as how much a "proper loaf" of bread should weigh.

To ascertain this important manufacturing intelligence the services of George Cabot, a prosperous businessman, were enlisted. Mr. Cabot, a merchant and shipowner, was involved in the cotton mills in Beverly, Massachusetts, and eventually became a U.S. senator. The task at hand — making inquiries into the nature of manufacturing in his home county of Essex — led him to the town of Ipswich, where Joseph Dana was selected to assist in the gathering of information. The reasons for his selection were varied. Having graduated from Yale in 1760,[7] Dana was educated and capable, as well as the respected and, by all accounts, well-liked pastor of the South Church. As an active member of the community, investing in the local manufacturing, he was knowledgeable about the town's commerce. His family was known for hosting spinning bees. Joseph Dana reports on two industries in Ipswich: cordage, in which he had investments,[8] and lace, which he defines in detail.

### A Dispersed Situation

Gathering the information requested turned out to be no small feat for Joseph Dana. He complained to Cabot: "So that to ascertain 'the quantity and value of the annual finished work' is an undertaking of some difficulty."[9] He explained that the making of lace was in a "dispersed situation" and involved no less than six hundred lace makers.

Dana's complaint posses an abundance of interesting questions. Why did the workers of this industry seem to be scattered all over the countryside? How were they organized? Why didn't George Cabot ask the persons in charge of the industry for this "intelligence" instead of a pastor who had no direct ties or even investments? How did a town of 4,500 people develop a population of 600 lace makers? Are Dana's figures embellished? Why did this industry develop in Ipswich and nowhere else?

### Finding the Answers

Answering these questions begins with an understanding of life in the eighteenth century, which was dramatically different from that of our world. In a time before factories, Ipswich had not yet established even its first bank. Currency was in very short supply. In general, business was conducted very differently from what we are accustomed to in the twenty-first century, with its mass production and electronic transactions. Dana's difficulty was caused by an array of circumstances, beginning with the reality that a large number of lace makers were scattered all over the local area.

## The Population

The population of Ipswich, according to the U.S. census of 1790, was 4,562 residents. Of those, 2,414 were female. According to Joseph Dana's records there were over six hundred women and girls making lace that year—25 percent of the total female population. The total female population would include newborns to the extremely old. Since census records for that year show only "free white females, including heads of families," it would be interesting to know how many of 2,414 females in Ipswich were either too young, too old, or too disabled to make lace. Such records do not exist, but it seems clear from those that are available that a significant number of the able female population in Ipswich was involved in the industry.

These figures do not mean that large numbers of women were leaving their homes and going to work every day. Because this was a time before factories, the place of commerce and industry was the home. That explains why the lace makers were in such a "dispersed situation": each lace maker was working out of her home, as would be expected. Even traveling workers, such as farmhands and tailors, went to individual homes to perform their trades. "Stores" were common additions to many households. A majority of the male population could be considered merchants, at least in some respects, as most were involved in selling goods or services.

The handmade-lace industry of Ipswich was a domestic industry in more than one sense. The lace was "domestic" because it was made on American soil. It also qualifies as a domestic product in the sense that the work was done in individual homes. In Ipswich lace making can be seen the beginning steps toward factories: the outwork industry of the machine-made laces of Ipswich. This industry was run by men, operating machines that produced a lacelike mesh. The mesh was sent home with women workers, who employed needle and thread to incorporate the design work into the mesh to make it look like lace, and the finished product was returned to the "manufactory." Outwork industries were the precursors of factories. Ipswich later developed factories such as those that produced knitted stockings.

Joseph Dana's difficulty in "ascertaining" the data explains why he was chosen instead of an agent or person in charge of the industry. He was chosen because there wasn't one individual or agent in charge of the industry who could provide the required data.

At the time of Joseph Dana lace making was a domestic industry run by women, not an outwork industry run by men. If there had been an agent or commission merchant, this agent rather than Dana would have been chosen to answer the request for information from the company's records. Joseph Dana had to enlist the women of his parish to go door-to-door and speak with each lace maker to determine how much lace she had made, what type it was, and what price it brought at market. During this process the samples of lace were collected that later became a part of his report.

There has been some question of whether the Rev. Mr. Dana exaggerated his findings, not an uncommon occurrence. He carefully noted that he had taken extra care to ensure the accuracy of his accounting. Evidence from other records supports his data in that the amount of lace and its selling price is realistic for the period. Also, the ratio of lace made per person is right on target. It would be unlikely that Joseph Dana would even have thought of this factor. This ratio is a subtle bit of information known to lace makers and of little consideration to others.

In support of his claim that every effort was made to ensure that the information obtained was accurate, Dana stated that "most of the [lace making] families were waited upon twice, by the young ladies who undertook this enquiry."[10] In a town of 600 lace makers and 602 dwellings, a large number of homes in Ipswich had at least one lace maker, making the visits to obtain the information an assiduous project. It took a year for Joseph Dana to obtain the information and make his report to George Cabot.

### The Town of Ipswich

The answers to why and how a lace-making industry developed in Ipswich lie within an understanding of the town itself. Originally named Agawam by Native Americans,[11] the town was renamed Ipswich on August 4, 1634, by British authority. By the eighteenth century it was a bustling administrative county seat, filled with the excitement of a busy seaport and dependent on importing, farming, and fishing. Ipswich came to rival Salem in both population and trade, especially import trade. Large ships routinely stopped at Ipswich to off-load their exotic treasures and long-awaited shipments of goods. They would then pick up raw materials, such as wood and tobacco, to take back to England. Many families depended on the import trade, either directly—like the Heard family, whose main profession was importing—or indirectly—like the Howe family, who were farmers and benefited by selling their goods to those who had become wealthy from such endeavors.

### Lost Trade

Beginning in the 1740s, the shifting sands at the mouth of the Ipswich River gradually closed the harbor to larger ships. This event was no surprise. The famous Captain John Smith wrote of his impression of the situation, "This place might content a right curious judgment; but there are many sands at the entrance of the harbour, and the worst is, it is imbayed too farre from the deepe sea."[12] Ipswich lost its import trade because the larger ships could no longer reach the harbor or even hope to get close enough to off-load their goods. In the *American Gazetteer*, 1797, Jedidiah Morse recalled, "This was heretofore a place of much more consideration than at present. Its decline is attributed to a barred harbour and shoals in the river. Its natural situation is pleasant, and on all accounts excellently well calculated to be a large manufacturing town." Even though small fishing boats continued their trade, the economic impact of the loss of imports had a ripple effect throughout the entire town, and by 1750 economic decline had an impact on the majority of the town's people.

### The Embargoes

Frustrations over taxation and trade issues began to arise between the colonists and England. The Stamp Act and embargoes caused further economic woes. The page shown in fig. 8 was printed in Boston in 1767. The "Resolutions of the Freeholders of Boston" reports, under "America," on the meeting of October 28, 1767, and the resulting decision to reject foreign goods. Notice that the ninth line from the bottom defines

## Resolutions of the Freeholders of Boston.

lency was pleased to return the following answer:

"I will, with the utmost expedition, as soon as it is in my power, transmit to Great Britain the heads of a bill for limiting the duration of parliaments; and I will, according to your desire, most faithfully represent them to his Majesty, as the general sense of the Commons of Ireland."

We hear that a bill hath passed the House of Commons, to lay a tax of four shillings in the pound upon all pensions, places, and employments, civil and military, upon all people who do not reside in this kingdom, and shall be absent for a limited time.

### A M E R I C A.

From the Boston (New England) Gazette, at the top of which is printed, in Italicks, *Save your Money, and you save your Country!*

*Boston, Nov.* 2. At a meeting of the freeholders and other inhabitants of the town of Boston, legally assembled at Faneuil-Hall, on Wednesday the 28th of October, 1767, the Hon. James Otis, Esq; moderator; a written address to the inhabitants, subscribed *Philo Patriæ*, recommending œconomy and manufactures, was, by their order, read:

The town then took into consideration the petition of a number of inhabitants, "That some effectual measures might be agreed upon to promote industry, œconomy, and manufactures; thereby to prevent the unnecessary importation of European commodities, which threaten the country with poverty and ruin;" whereupon in a very large and full meeting, the following votes and resolutions were passed unanimously:

Whereas the excessive use of foreign superfluities is the chief cause of the present distressed state of this town, as it is thereby drained of its money; which misfortune is likely to be increased by means of the late additional burthens and impositions on the trade of the province, which threaten the country with poverty and ruin:

Therefore, voted, That this town will take all prudent and legal measures to encourage the produce and manufactures of this province, and to lessen the use of superfluities, and particularly the following enumerated articles imported from abroad, viz. loaf sugar, cordage, anchors, coaches, chaises, and carriages of all sorts, horse furniture, men and women's hats, men's and women's apparel ready made, household furniture, gloves, men's and women's shoes, sole-leather, sheathing and deck nails, gold and silver and thread lace of all sorts, gold and silver buttons, wrought plate of all sorts, diamonds, stone and paste ware, snuff, mustard, clocks and watches, silversmiths and jewellers ware, broad cloths that cost above 10s. per yard, muffs, furrs, and tippets, and all sorts of millenery ware, starch, women's and children's stays, fire-engines, china ware, silk and cotton velvets, gauze, pewterers hollow ware, linseed oil, glue, lawns, cambricks, silks of all kinds for garments, malt liquors and cheese. And that a subscription for this end be and hereby is recommended to the several inhabitants and housholders of the town; and that John Rowe, Esq; Mr. William Greenleafe, Meletiah Bourne, Esq; Mr. Samuel Austin, Mr. Edward Payne, Mr. Edmund Quincy, John Ruddock, Esq; Jonathan Williams, Esq; Joshua Henshaw, Esq; Mr. Henderson Inches, Mr. Solomon Davis, Joshua Winslow, Esq; and Thomas Cushing, Esq; be a committee to prepare a form for subscription, to report the same as soon as possible; and also to procure subscriptions to the same.

And whereas it is the opinion of this town, that divers new manufactures may be set up in America, to its great advantage, and some others carried to a greater extent, particularly those of glass and paper.

Therefore, voted, That this town will, by all prudent ways and means, encourage the use and consumption of glass and paper, made in any of the British American colonies; and more especially in this province.

Then the meeting adjourned till 3 o'clock in the afternoon; when the committee appointed in the forenoon, to prepare a form for subscription, reported as follows:

Whereas this province labours under a heavy debt, incurred in the course of the late war; and the inhabitants by this means must be for some time subject to very burthensome taxes; and as our trade has for some years been on the decline, and is now particularly under great embarrassments, and burthened with heavy impositions, our medium very scarce, and the balance of trade greatly against this country:

We therefore the subscribers, being sensible that it is absolutely necessary, in order to extricate us out of these embarrassed and distressed circumstances, to promote industry, œconomy, and manufactures among ourselves, and by this means prevent the unnecessary importation of European commodities, the excessive use of which threatens the country with poverty and ruin, do promise and engage, to and with each other, that we will encourage the use and consumption of all articles manufactured in any of the British American colonies, and more especially in this province; and that we will not, from and after the 31st day of December next ensuing, purchase any of the following articles imported from abroad, viz. loaf sugar, and all the other articles enumerated above.

And we further agree strictly to adhere to the late regulation respecting funerals, and will not use any gloves but what are manufactured here, nor procure any new garments upon such an occasion, but what shall be absolutely necessary.

The above report having been considered, the question was put, Whether the same shall "gold and silver and thread lace of all sorts." This document and many others like it verify that the purchases of imported goods such as lace, tea, loaf sugar, hats, and many other items were discouraged.

The embargoes against English goods of all sorts, specifically luxury items such as tea and lace, began in the 1760s. On March 19, 1770, Ipswich followed Boston's lead and voted to join in the movement to reject imported goods.

> We are determined to retrench all extravagances, and that we will, to the utmost of our power, encourage our own manufactures, and that we will not, by ourselves or any for or under us, directly or indirectly purchase any goods of the persons who have imported or continue to import, or of any person or trader, who shall purchase any goods of said importer contrary to the agreement of the merchants in Boston and the other trading towns in this government and the neighboring colonies, until they make a public retraction, or a general importation takes place. And, further, taking under consideration the excessive use of tea, which has been such a bane to this country, voted, that we will abstain therefrom ourselves, and recommend the disuse of it in our families, until all the revenue acts are repealed.[13]

Reading of these strong sentiments, one might think that the purchase of all imported goods stopped upon agreements like the ones in Ipswich and Boston. However, even though most towns passed such statements, in reality imported goods continued to be available in American markets and were purchased by some segments of the population. The purchase of these goods had a lot to do with political views, economic situation, and social standing. In some cases it was simply a matter of taste: a warm cup of tea was still an enticing comfort.

*The American Revolution*

The conflict with England finally produced the American Declaration of Independence and war with England. The economic consequences for the average citizen were a heavy burden. Men were torn between pursuing their professions, caring for their land and families, and fighting for independence. Abigail Adams, like many women, suffered long separations from her husband, John Adams. She wrote to him of her heartfelt loss: "You tell me you know not when you shall see me. I never trust myself long with the terrors which sometimes intrude themselves upon me."[14]

The terrors of war were more than enough for these women who had to make life-changing decisions and try to clothe and feed their families without the support and comfort of their husbands. Abigail again writes: "We live in Continual Expectation of Hostilities." She inquires if Congress understands their situation, "Does every Member feel for us? Can they realize what we suffer? And can they believe with what patience and fortitude we endure the conflict?"[15]

Complicating matters were numerous outbreaks of disease such as smallpox. After surviving an early form of inoculations for smallpox, which, though they were meant to build resistance to the disease, usually made people sick, Abigail wrote, "All my treasure of children have passed thro one of the most terrible Diseases to which humane Nature is subject, and not one of us is wanting."[16] Not all could report such joyous news.

The women of Ipswich would have understood these words. They too saw their men gather in groups and march off to war. They too lived in fear of smallpox and the possible loss of their spouses and children or even their homes. The Old Burying Ground at Ipswich is filled with tiny graves of children and infants who died of disease or simply failed to thrive during this period.

Women were often left to care for the family and the land and to keep shops and enterprises going while their husbands and sons were gone for extended periods of time. It was not uncommon for a young woman to be left to care for her younger siblings and herself because of the loss of a father and mother to disease or the war. Natalie S. Bober, in her book on Abigail Adams, writes, "With John away, Abigail tried to keep her family fed, clothed, and out of debt. She wove her own cloth and made all the family's clothes. She did this not only in an effort to keep expenses down, but also as a matter of patriotism. Abigail and her friends believed that women's efforts on the home front were essential to ensure the ultimate success of the American cause."[17] Staying out of debt had long been part of the struggle of the women of Ipswich.

*Ipswich Responds*

Ipswich seems to have embraced orders to encourage homespun "manufacturys." The desire to support both community and family was the driving force behind the lace industry. Fashion and the demand for lace provided the market. Lace making allowed women the opportunity to

*Fig. 9.* Account of David Pulsipher and his promise to pay in lace, from the account book of Ezekial Dodge, an Ipswich dry goods merchant, June 11, 1768. *Dodge Account Book. Photograph courtesy Peabody Essex Museum.*

strengthen their family's economic situation. For some it was a significant source of income; for others it was a supplemental source.

The 1768 account book of Ezekiel Dodge[18] (fig. 9), a dry goods merchant in Ipswich, records a debt owed to him by David Pulcipher for the purchase of chintz:

> 1768
> June 11      to 5 yd chince
>              N. B. lase is to be paid for
>              the chince in 5 weeks from /date.

*N.B.* is an abbreviation for *nota bene*, meaning "take note" or "this is important." Mr. Dodge was making a note to remind himself that lace was owed to him as payment for the debt. What is even more interesting about this entry is that the gentleman purchasing the chintz needed five weeks to return with the lace in hand. In all likelihood he needed the five weeks for the women in his household to produce the lace to pay the debt. The cost of the chintz was one pound, three shillings, four pence. This would have been a comfortable debt to pay with lace valued at approximately eighteen shillings per yard.

According to surviving account books, Mr. Pulcipher was a regular customer. He had accounts with several other Ipswich merchants, including Timothy Bragg. During the time when he was paying his debts with lace, he was also routinely purchasing large amounts of "quality thread." On August 4, 1768, Mr. Pulcipher (or Pulcifer, depending on how each merchant preferred to spell his name) bought two more skeins of thread for two shillings, six pence. Since lace is made from this thread, such purchases indicate that this household was engaged in lace making.

Lace making began as a handy way for women to contribute to the family's economic situation. In some households that meant being able to pay down debts or purchase staples. In others it meant being able to buy occasional luxuries. In either case, lace allowed families to obtain goods that would otherwise have been just outside their economic capabilities. One can easily understand the excitement of being able to purchase silk for a new dress, velvet for a cape, or even snuff during a time of such hardship, when merely obtaining enough food to eat and paper to write on was a challenge.

Maintaining the family required the efforts of all members be available as quickly as possible. Traditionally, children began to learn how to wind thread onto the bobbins as young as four years of age. A productive lace maker could be as young as eight or nine years or as mature as 90 years of age. The town's many lace makers spanned a wide range of ages. However, Ipswich did not acquire these six hundred lace makers overnight.

Developing competent lace makers in such numbers took time and determination. The women were motivated to keep their families together and to help maintain the highest standard of living possible. Lace making flourished in Ipswich because it provided some economic relief during the years of trade losses and disputes, conflicts over taxation, and battles with England. And it had many attractive advantages that made it easy to make and sell: it could be made by both the young and the elderly, it could be made at home with simple tools, and many yards of it could easily be taken to market, where it would fetch a handsome price.

Because the women involved in the industry were either descendants of settlers from England or were from there themselves, it was natural that their little industry would be closely modeled on lace-making industries in England. "The English lace industry, in common with those of the Continent, was a cottage industry dependent on the labour of women and children and it was closely associated with poor relief."[19] In many ways it was like its English counterpart in that it was a cottage or domestic industry in which women and girls did the work. Ipswich operated with a few very notable exceptions to the English system. Because lace making is customarily the trade of poorer women, the unexpected discovery that women in moderate social standing were making lace in Ipswich raised more than a few eyebrows. However, when understood in its historical context, this surprising twist makes sense. It is likely that economic pressures attracted these women to the trade that they might quietly maintain the standard of living that had been their custom. Or they may have been motivated, as was Abigail Adams, to support "the cause" and show their patriotism by their involvement in the industry.

Lace making was attractive in that it could be practiced discreetly. Lace could be made in the home by any number of people living there, and it could go to market with the head of the household, as in the case of Mr. Pulcipher, or be passed on to one of the women who collected the lace once a week and took it to market. Much like weaving, it was a clever and tactful way for a father to put his girls to work without seeming to employ them. Putting girls to work would have been frowned on, especially for girls from families in higher social rankings. These girls could easily have earned their own dowries in this manner, saving the household a considerable expense.

*Homemade versus Imported*

By the time of the embargoes, the number of lace makers in Ipswich was growing. As in every other town, women and girls in Ipswich did spinning, weaving, and sewing, normal routines of life in the colonies. Most colonists were not accustomed to buying their clothes ready-made. However, the commodity of lace was a different story. Even though the skill of lace making was not uncommon, most lace was worn by the wealthy who did not make lace themselves but rather were the driving force in the demand for lace. The lace these women desired was ready-made and imported. The French, Flemish, and Brussels laces were the most highly sought after and were worn by women of the highest social and economic levels. Large amounts of English lace were also imported for children's clothing, women's caps and handkerchiefs. But the embargoes and conflicts changed the dynamics of the lace trade. More lace began to be made and sold at home instead of being imported ready-made. The women of

Ipswich adapted their routines and seized the market generated by the clashes with England and the economic opportunities that lace making provided.

The Ipswich women discovered the benefits lace making could bring. As it was in high demand, everyone knew its market value. It was light and could easily be rolled up into a small parcel and taken to market. When corn would bring in only two or three shillings a bushel, lace brought in eighteen shillings or more per yard. Lace could be made any time of year, and it could be picked up or put down as needed. The trade of lace was convenient and economically rewarding. Because Ipswich went through an economic decline and financial pressure before the other towns around them, it was prepared for the market demands for lace when the embargoes and even tougher times came later.

By 1776 the number of lace makers in Ipswich was so large that, unlike other areas, the residents were poised to meet the demand for domestic lace brought on by the war. By a twist of fate, when the market for American lace presented itself, Ipswich was already in full production and was able to produce the volume of lace necessary to meet the demand. Ipswich had the good fortune to be in the right place at the right time with the right numbers of lace makers.

The anti-English sentiment brought on by war had a serious impact on the lace trade of the English Midlands. Before the American Revolution, the English colonies were the single largest importer of English lace. The war disrupted this trade. Santina Levey, in her book *Lace: A History*, speaks of the effects of the war on the lace makers of the Midlands: "The decline in the English industry began during the American War of Independence (1773–82) which destroyed the main overseas market" (p. 59). She also notes that a curiously large amount of lace thread was exported from London to Boston in the second half of the eignteenth century. One wonders if the English knew what the Americans were doing with all that English lace thread.

After the war, America was in debt. Economic stresses continued as a new country tried to absorb the cost of war. The lace industry continued because it created a product in high demand, and it continued to afford economic benefits to the lace makers who were in need of financial relief. The moderate price range of the lace made it available for the first time to the middle and upper-middle class. And considering the influence of fashion, this was a very attractive option for many women. A period of economic growth began in 1790 that carried the lace industry into the nineteenth century; it continued until changes in fashion and the invention of the lace machines forever changed the market for lace.

Therefore, the industry of handmade lace in Ipswich came about through several factors that converged at one time and place. Lace making was the Ipswich answer to economic decline. Fashion and politics provided a market for the lace. Social changes allowed women the opportunity to sell lace beyond the bounds of their hometown. Ipswich had the good fortune to have enough people with the right skills to take advantage of the times and the market.

*The Lace and Its Market Value*

The scope of Joseph Dana's work is impressive, considering that he had to obtain detailed information that was known only to six hundred individual lace makers scattered throughout the area. The record he left behind reports on the actual value of the lace at market.

Joseph Dana's inquiry shows that much of the lace was sold directly from the lace makers' pillows. Even more was taken to markets and traded for goods. When the lace was traded to a merchant, it was sold at a discount, and the merchant earned a profit by selling the lace at the full market value or at the "dealer's markup." An excellent example of this markup can be found in the account book of Timothy Brag, dry goods merchant in Ipswich.[20] On December 18, 1767, the account of Thomas Hodgskins is reckoned as follows: "Thomas Hodgskins, *wife*," pays the account "by 3¾ [yards] bone lace" at eighteen shillings per yard. A transaction on July 16, 1768, records that Timothy Brag purchased ¾ yards of the lace at twenty shillings per yard.[21] Because this merchant did not usually deal in lace it is very clear that he received Mrs. Hodgskins's lace at one price and sold it to himself for a higher price. (Merchants were often their own best customers. Many account books have been identified by examining whose account was the most vigorous.) In the same account book a Mr. Stephen Burnam, son of Stephen, also purchased ¾ yards of lace, also at twenty shillings per yard.

The Reverend Mr. Dana reflects this markup in his accounting when listing each type of lace sold over the year, its price by the yard, and the total sums for each type sold, computing the grand total as 41,979 yards of lace and edging, sold at 1,869 pounds, 8 shillings, 10 pence.[22] (See fig. 5.) Dana made a deduction to show the value of the lace without the dealers' markup. He explained, "For the Stock [the lace] computed at the rates at which it is usually purchased—it is supposed there must be a deduction of about one Third from the price of the lace—Call it £600—And the sum left is £1,269.8.10."[23]

### Changes in Organization

The documented production and sale of 41,979 yards of lace in a single year became a notable achievement that was reflected in other publications, such as the *American Gazetteer*, by Jedidiah Morse. He states: "Silk and thread lace, of an elegant texture, are manufactured here by women and children, in large quantities, and sold for use and exportation in Boston and other mercantile towns. In 1790, no less than 41,979 yards were made here, and the manufacture is rather increasing."[24] By 1797, Ipswich lace was a small industry that had gained some recognition. The reports of Joseph Dana gave the industry a new distinction, that of the potential for profitability. There is much evidence, which will be discussed in later chapters, that as businessmen recognized the potential for profits they became involved in the industry. Just after Dana's report, the industry shows clear signs of becoming more organized, which in all likelihood meant that commission merchants got involved. At this point the industry changed from a domestic industry loosely organized by women to the more organized, male-dominated mainstream world of business. This change coincided with the growing economy and the great pride the country took in American-made products at the beginning of the nineteenth century.

### Machine-made Lace

By 1821 machines for making lace had been introduced into the United States, and the Boston & Ipswich Lace Company was incorporated in 1824. It was actually the netting that was done by machine. Men ran the machines, and women "flowered," or embroidered, the lace designs on the net to look like handmade laces. This type of outwork industry was a precursor to what we understand as a factory. As machine laces streamed into American markets, the American handmade-lace industry suffered. England was experiencing the same shift from handmade to machine-made lace during this period. Fashions had changed. Lace, once a symbol of wealth, lost its social prestige, having been replaced by machine laces that were available to almost anyone. Within two decades the production of handmade lace in Ipswich gradually declined from a domestic industry to a domestic pastime. There is evidence that the two industries coexisted, at least for a time, and that some women worked in both. Mary Ann Jewett, one of the Ipswich lace makers, was reported to have two famous sisters, Hannah and Harriet. Known as the the Jewett twins, they worked in the machine lace industry. The industry of handmade lace in Ipswich began around 1750, went into a gradual decline beginning in the early 1820s, and had ended by the 1840s.

*A New Era, the Nineteenth Century*

The lace pillow of Helen Choate, owned by the Society for the Preservation of New England Antiquities (see fig. 10), had several owners and continued to be used well into the nineteenth century. This pillow can be described as a "classic" of Ipswich lace making. Filled with saltwater marsh grasses, the inner fabric is homespun linen, the pricking is of a pattern common to the industry, and the bobbins are also typical.

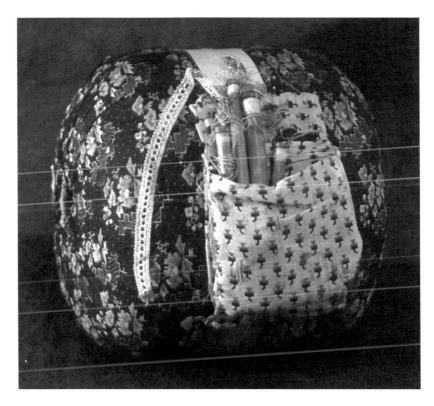

*Fig. 10.* The lace on Helen Choate's pillow exemplifies one of the most commonly made patterns of the Ipswich industry. *Lace maker's pillow. 1810–1840. Gift of Helen Choate, 1943.479. Society for the Preservation of New England Antiquities.*

Discovered in a pocket on this pillow was a card for the Choates'
Ipswich and Boston Express, a railroad service between Ipswich and
Boston (see fig. 11). Before the railroad the stage was the mode of transportation used to move lace and many other goods to market. Because of
the relatively large number of passengers seeking travel to mercantile
towns, the people of Ipswich eagerly awaited the opening of the railroad.
"Senate Document No. 77 of 1836, . . . reported: Stage passengers from
Ipswich to Boston were 2,000."[25] The first rail service triumphantly came
to Ipswich on Friday, December 20, 1839. The fare to Boston was 87½
cents.[26]

There had been much social, political, and economic change in Ipswich
since the mid-1700s. However, samples of Ipswich lace documented as
having been made in 1880 and later confirm that a few women continued
to make lace for the rest of their lives, long after the industry of handmade lace was over.

*An Industry Remembered*

Knowledge of the lace industry was kept alive by the descendants of the
Ipswich lace makers, most notably Sarah E. Lakeman and Mabel Foster
Bainbridge. The Colonial Revival played a part in reviving interest in the
industry and in lace making in general; this interest continued until the

1940s. Many curators and collectors of the early twentieth century also helped to preserve the history of lace making.

## I. INTRODUCTION

1. Fortunately there are a few notable exceptions. One of these exceptions is *A Midwife's Tale: The Life of Martha Ballard, Based on Her Diary, 1785–1812*, by Laurel Thatcher Ulrich (New York: Alfred A. Knopf, 1990; reprint, New York: Vintage Books, 1991). This remarkable work is an insightful study into the daily lives of eighteenth-century women. The story is told through the life and times of Martha Ballard, based on her own diary. Laurel Thatcher Ulrich is a master of social history and historical research. Her work is well worth reading.

Another recommended work on the topic of women's lives is *Abigail Adams, Witness to a Revolution*, by Natalie S. Bober (New York: Aladdin Paperbacks, 1998). Abigail Adams was a prolific writer who showed great interest in the political world that surrounded her. This work explores her life experiences as recorded in her letters and diaries.

2. Richard M. Candee, "Lace Schools and Lace Factories: Female Outwork in New England's Machine-Lace Industry, 1818–1838," in the *Dublin Seminar for Early New England Folklife* (1997), vol. 22, *Textiles in Early New England: Design, Production, and Consumption* (Boston: Boston University Press, 1999), pp. 100–26.

3. Joseph Dana to George Cabot, July 26, 1790, and January 24, 1791, Papers of Alexander Hamilton, Manuscript Department, Library of Congress, Washington, D.C. (hereafter Hamilton Papers). Also see Arthur Harrison Cole, ed., *Industrial and Commercial Correspondence of Alexander Hamilton, Anticipating His Report on Manufactures* (New York: Augustus M. Kelley, 1968), pp. 54–55, for published letters of Joseph Dana.

4. The letters of Joseph Dana are just as rare and valuable as the lace. As an interesting note to paper conservationists, these letters happen to bear every method of paper conservation ever used in this country.

5. Joseph Dana to George Cabot, January 24, 1791, Hamilton Papers, p. 1.

6. Seven inches is a rough average calculated from the approximate number of lace makers in Ipswich and the total yardage made that same year. Some of the narrow or simpler laces took less time; the wider and more complicated laces would have been more time-intensive to produce.

7. Joseph Dana later went on to receive a doctorate of divinity from Harvard in 1801.

8. Cordage is the manufacture of roping, especially the type used in ship rigging. Joseph Dana notes in his letter of July 26, 1790, to George Cabot (Hamilton Papers) that he has investments in the cordage industry.

9. Dana to Cabot, July 26, 1790, Hamilton Papers.

10. Dana to Cabot, January 24, 1791, Hamilton Papers.

11. The Ipswich Historical Society has preserved much of the early artifacts and evidence of interactions between Native Americans and the first settlers. Their collections include shells, tomahawks, gouges, pestles and mortars, and arrowheads.

12. Joseph B. Felt, *History of Ipswich, Essex, and Hamilton* (Cambridge, Mass., 1834; reprint, Ipswich, Mass.: Clamshell Press, 1966), p. 36.

13. Felt, *History of Ipswich, Essex, and Hamilton*, p. 130.

14. Natalie S. Bober, *Abigail Adams: Witness to a Revolution*, (New York: Aladdin Paperbacks, 1998), p. 56.

15. Ibid.

16. Ibid., p. 78.

17. Ibid., p. 81

18. Account book of Ezekiel Dodge, beginning in 1767, Peabody Essex Museum, Salem, Mass.

19. Santina M. Levey, *Lace: A History* (London: W. S. Maney & Son for Victoria and Albert Museum, 1983), p. 59.

20. Timothy Bragg, Account Book, 3 vols., 1767, Heard House Archive, Account Books and Manuscripts, Ipswich Historical Society, Ipswich, Mass.

21. Ibid.

22. Enclosure, Dana to Cabot, January 24, 1791.

23. Ibid.

24. Jedidiah Morse, *The American Gazetteer*, (Charlestown, Mass., 1797), pp. IPS–IRO.

25. Thomas Franklin Waters, *Ipswich in Massachusetts Bay Colony, 1700–1917* (Ipswich, Mass.: Ipswich Historical Society, 1917), 2:588.

26. Ibid.

# TOOLS OF THE TRADE

*From the Most Humble of Tools Is Wrought a Thing of Exceptional Beauty*

WHEN COMPARING the simplicity of the tools used to make lace with the finished product, it is hard to imagine that such a delicate and intricate fabric could possibly come from such unpretentious tools. These modest tools are recorded in Joseph Dana's letter dated July 26, 1790. He described the simplicity of the "machinery" used to make lace, "consisting only of a round or perhaps elliptical pillow, from 8 to 12 inches diameter; a strip of parchment or paste-board, encircling the same,—(upon which the pattern of the lace is pricked out)—a few rows of pins; and bobbins—from a dozen to 120, according to the width & figure of the pattern."[1] This document is an accurate list of the tools used in the making of bobbin lace.

To understand the significance of the artifacts of this industry it is important to know a little bit about lace making. Bobbin lace is made on what is called a lace pillow, a solid foundation on which lace is made (see fig. 12). It is a platform that can securely hold the pins and lace in place during production. The lace is made from thread wound on bobbins. The lace is worked over a template-like pattern called a pricking. Think of lace making as weaving in miniature, with the pins holding the threads in place as the stitches are worked.

The pillow is held in the lap, on a stand designed to hold lace pillows, which is sometimes called a horse, or it is simply rested on the edge of a table. The lace maker then crosses and twists the threads to produce the desired design. The tools to produce bobbin lace can vary greatly in size, style, color, and sophistication.

The tools used in the Ipswich industry are standard for lace making in general but distinctive to Ipswich because of the characteristics of the materials used and the methods and markings of their construction. These features differentiate them from other lace-making tools used elsewhere. The tools also show evidence that they were not used by a hobbyist, nor were they the possession of a few individuals who were making lace for their own purposes. These tools were clearly intended for the hard work of industry.

*Fig. 12.* Lace pillow of Mrs. N. H. Lord, of Ipswich, Massachusetts. *Courtesy, Ipswich Historical Society, Ipswich, Massachusetts.*

Such tools demonstrate a conservation of materials typical of items made for use in an industry. Each was made by hand from inexpensive materials and resources readily available to anyone in the Ipswich area. They were purposeful objects, made with the intention of producing as much lace as possible and doing so as quickly and as economically as possible. They are without pretension, neither treasured gifts nor mementos.

Of the items used in the industry and described by Joseph Dana, the only supplies that were purchased rather than homemade were the pins and thread. Both of these items were imported and could be purchased at local markets and in the mercantile towns around Ipswich.

*Pins*

Pins, important for making clothing and lace, had to be imported because they were not made in the colonies; in fact, they were not made in America until the one-piece pin became available in the 1830s. During the early and most active years of the industry, pins were individually handmade and therefore expensive. Each pin was cut from wire and individually sharpened; then the head of each pin was applied, one at a time (see fig. 13). Such a labor-intensive process accounts for the high cost and short supply, especially as tensions rose with England. The resulting trade disputes made the availability of pins sporadic at best. The ideal type of pin for lace making had to be smooth, strong, and very fine. They were an even harder treasure to find than regular sewing pins.

## Pin Money

Because the ideal pins for lace making were impossible to find, most women settled for what was available. The ability to adapt seems to be one of the foremost survival tools for those who lived in eighteenth-century America. Abigail Adams, who was a prolific writer, often requested a "bundle of pins" from her husband, John Adams, when he was away on long journeys. Mr. Adams, who was elected as the second president of the United States in 1797, spent much time away from home. A week after the conflict at Concord and Lexington on April 19, 1775, John Adams traveled to Philadelphia as a delegate to the Second Continental Congress. Even though Abigail was close enough to Boston to take advantage of the markets there, she took the opportunity offered by John's travels to request that he send pins, telling him that the "cry" for pins is "great."[2] Pins were a cherished item that women guarded with care.

Pins, modern or ancient, are easily lost and require some sort of con-

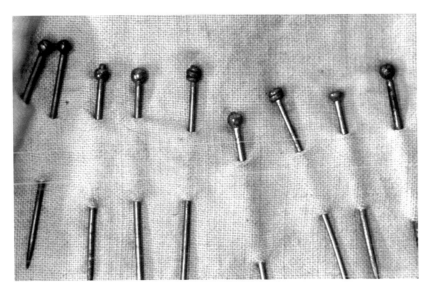

*Fig. 13.* Small package of handmade pins. *NN (no accession number). Society for the Preservation of New England Antiquities.*

tainer to store them. The value of objects can sometimes be determined by how they are cared for and what type of container is used to protect them. The mass-produced pins of today are often stored in paper cards or plastic boxes that are inexpensive and easily broken. By comparison the handmade pins of the eighteenth century were securely held in beautiful pin holders or pin cases that reflected their worth.

As an example of their value, pin holders were often given as gifts to show friendship, gratitude, or respect. These cases were frequently hand-made, with creative and elaborate needlework designs. The effort expended to create these tiny containers reflects the importance of each precious pin. Women seemed to have a continuing regard for their supply of pins. The term "pin money" came from the practice of saving up money whenever possible for the purchase of pins. Pins cost six shillings, eight pence per thousand in 1543[3] and ten shillings by the late seventeenth century.[4] According to Judith Reiter Weissman and Wendy Lavitt, in their book *Labors of Love*, in the late 1600s a small packet of a dozen pins listed in inventories of Massachusetts had a value equal to a bedstead! By the time of the American Revolution pins became even more scarce because of the conflict with England.

To Pin or Not to Pin

In a culture of hand sewing, needlework, and lace making it is easy to understand the value of a "bundle of pins." Pins are vital in lace making because they hold the threads in place while the lace is being made. There are many reports in old texts of women resorting to fish bones in desperate times. Lace makers adapted their techniques to use as few pins as possible, in part because of the expense. Using fewer pins had the added benefit of faster work, as it takes time to push in a pin at each stitch. Lace makers found that they could make the background mesh, or ground-work, of the lace without pins. Even today most accomplished lace makers can construct basic groundwork stitches without the use of pins.

One of the characteristics of prickings used in lace making during the industry is the absence of pinholes in the groundwork areas. All ground-work in the narrow laces was made without pins. But the prickings for the wider black laces did provide holes for the groundwork stitches. The reason may have been simply practicality. The wider laces were made from silk, which is slippery. The use of pins in the groundwork makes the handling of the silk threads more manageable. The wider laces also had more ground-work space to deal with, which makes the use of pins worth the effort.

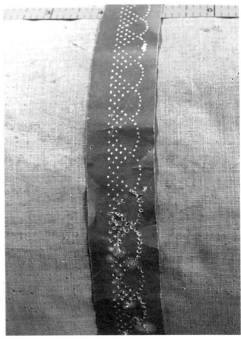

*Fig. 15.* Blueprint pricking, ca. 1930–1940, used by lace makers in one of the revivals of lace making in Ipswich, with pinholes in the areas of the groundwork. *Courtesy, Ipswich Historical Society, Ipswich, Massachusetts.*

*Fig. 14.* Parchment pricking used in the Ipswich lace industry, ca. 1800–1810, lacking pinholes in the areas of the groundwork. *Courtesy, Ipswich Historical Society, Ipswich, Massachusetts.*

The distinction between lace making as a hobby for personal use and lace making as an industry for commercial venture is very important. The industry began in the 1750s and continued into the 1840s. This distinction between industry and personal use can be seen in the prickings and the laces themselves. The old prickings from Ipswich reflect many of the differences between these periods. During the industry the groundwork was most often worked without pins. During later periods of hobby or personal use the groundwork has pins added.

Within this distinction between grounds that use pins and those that do not lies an interesting clue as to the differences between lace made in Ipswich during the industry and lace made later. The pricking shown in fig. 14 was used in the industry. Notice the triangles between the fan shapes and compare it to the twentieth-century pricking in figure 15. The twentieth-century pricking, circa 1939, was used in Ipswich during one of the lace-making revivals. A small piece of course cotton lace can be matched to this pricking and a few other prickings identical to it. This evidence shows a clear attempt to reproduce lace of the type made during the industry. Notice that pin holes have been added to the groundwork of the more modern prickings used during the Colonial Revival. Not only is there a difference in the way the groundwork is made, but you can also observe that the materials used in making these two prickings are very different. The pricking from the industry is made of parchment, but the pricking from the twentieth century is from a blueprint process that was not available until around 1930.

An additional note of interest for lace makers is that the laces made in this fan pattern during the lace industry period had eight pinholes on the edge of each fan (counting from the pinhole in the "valley" between the fans to the valley and pinhole that begins the next fan), whereas the ones from the Colonial Revival up to the late 1930s had ten pinholes along the edge. Also notice that the pricking used in the industry is well worn, and the hobby pricking was only partially used. Some of its pinholes have never even been pricked, which indicates that only a few inches of lace were made and then the effort was abandoned. This is common of hobby lace makers. They will try out a pattern or type of stitch until they learn it, and then they move on to something else. By contrast the professional lace makers made yards of the same lace over and over again.

### Thread

Ipswich lace was made of several different types of thread, depending on the period. The types of threads and fibers available for making lace changed from the early period of the industry, in the mid-eighteenth century, to the last years of the industry, in the early nineteenth century. Linen, or "thread,"[5] was used for lace making in the eighteenth century. Fashion gave rise to the use of silk to produce the soft, light, black laces for the shawls that were popular during the neoclassical period of the late eighteenth century. Lace for ladies' caps and children's clothing continued to be made from white linen thread. Improvements in spinning and processing techniques brought about the use of cotton threads for lace making in the 1820s. The use of the cotton thread became so popular that shortly after 1820 nearly all lace, machine-made and handmade, was made with cotton.

### Linen

The earliest Ipswich laces were made with a linen thread that would be very fine (325–250 wt.) by today's standards, although much finer threads

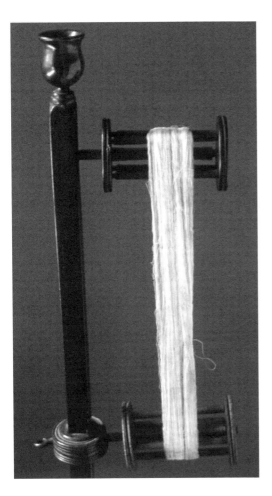

*Fig. 16.* Thread spindle from Ipswich. *Courtesy, Ipswich Historical Society, Ipswich, Massachusetts.*

were available in the later part of the eighteenth century. Linen comes from the fibers, known as flax, of the plant *Linum usitatissimum*. After a lengthy and tedious processing these fibers are spun into very fine thread. Flax is one of the longer (5–20 inches)[6] naturally occurring fibers used to spin thread. *Flax* refers to the fibers, and *linen* refers to a thread or fabric made from flax fibers.[7] Under microscopic examination linen thread looks similar to bamboo in that it has regular notches, called nodes. Linen thread was both very fine and strong.

## Silk

Laces made of black silk were exceptionally popular in the eighteenth century. When black lace shawls became popular, Ipswich responded by making its own version of a wide black silk lace designed to be competitive in the marketplace. American women of this period often had their portraits painted while wearing shawls made from Ipswich black silk lace or similar imported varieties, such as Blonde Lace, Bayeux, and Chantilly of France. Silk threads are made from the very long filament (915–3000 cm.)[8] that comes from the cocoons of the silkworm. Each cocoon is one long filament that when unwound can be spun into thread. Microscopic examination shows a filament that is very smooth with a subtle anomaly left from the points of contact with the cocoon. The silk thread used in Ipswich laces was hand-spun, was very soft to the touch, and was dyed black before it was made into lace. The softness of the thread indicates that it was boiled to remove the gum, or sericin. When the sericin is left in, the threads are much stiffer.

## Cotton

Linen and silk continued to be used into the nineteenth century. According to Santina Levey in written communication with the author, "Fine-spun English cotton thread was not adopted by lace makers until after the invention, by Samuel Hall in 1817, of the gassing technique, which burnt off the fluffy 'hairs' of the cotton. Its use then spread very rapidly. It was used for the machine-made net grounds in the Belgium industry almost immediately and was taken up by many hand-lace makers by the early 1820s." By the 1820s nearly all laces in Ipswich were made from cotton. This cotton thread, of exceedingly fine weight, was spun as a two-ply thread with an *S* twist. Cotton has much shorter fibers (0.75–5.8 cm)[9] than silk or linen and is not as strong as those threads. Under microscopic examination cotton looks much like translucent twisted ribbons.

## Imported Thread

There has been much debate over the question of whether Ipswich produced its own thread. While it is true that New England was known for its flax production, there is no evidence that the residents were able to spin thread of the fineness required for lace making. It takes an extraordinary amount of skill to spin thread that is pliable, strong, and fine enough for lace making. Spinners in Ipswich spun wool, flax, and hemp into heavier threads and yarns for weaving fabrics. The skill of the spinners of Ipswich would have compared to just about any in New England. Many were accomplished at spinning, and others were novices. But the purpose of their spinning was to make fabrics for use as towels, shirts, and shifts and heavier fabrics of wool for winter. The fabrics that remain today were made from the heavier homespun threads. Even the finest "home-grown" cloth was made from threads far too heavy for lace making; the finer linen and cotton threads had to be imported from England and France. It is interesting to note that, in their account books, American merchants often referred to lace thread as "quality thread" to emphasize its superior fineness. This thread was also more expensive.

The origin of silk thread is not so clear as that of the cotton and linen threads. China was not the only source for silk threads. France and Spain, which obtained their raw silk from China, were noted for their silk laces and threads. Newspaper advertisements from this period commonly announce the sale of imported silk thread or silk sewing thread from France. This was a strong thread appropriate for lace making and available in a variety of colors, including black. Such advertisements suggest that the threads used in making the black Ipswich lace were imported primarily from France.

The question of where this silk came from led many to wonder if the silk was domestically produced along with the lace. Certainly, there were many attempts, some quite vigorous, to produce domestic silk. One record states, "Fine samples of sewing Silk were also made in parts of Massachusetts, among others by Mr. Jones, of Western, in Worcester County, in 1790."[10] Many such accounts started with grand declarations and then did not last for a significant period of time. There are no records that suggest that silk production played an active part of Ipswich manufacturing. An interesting advertisement from long after the lace industry of Ipswich had faded was found in *The Queen*, the ladies' newspaper and court chronicle, of August 18, 1866: "Silk worms. Could you inform me of any place in London or elsewhere where I could dispose of 1500 healthy silkworms, good size, which have all been fed on mulberry and what price I could get for them?"[11] Whether in London or Massachusetts, silk production in general did rather poorly because of problems of climate and cultivating the required mulberry trees.

Many of the efforts at silk production came after silk thread laces had become a staple of the Ipswich lace industry. At the time that Ipswich was making black lace, there was a strong tradition of black lace making in Europe, which exported both the silk thread and finished laces to the colonies. Such thread regularly appeared in advertisements by most dry goods and sundries merchants. Whether Ipswich used domestic or imported silk thread or some of each will remain a question.

*Fig. 17.* Ipswich lace pillow used in the Ipswich lace industry, probably by a girl. The lace, a pattern often used by beginners, was made of very fine linen thread, ca. 1795–1820. Pins are handmade. *Courtesy, Ipswich Historical Society, Ipswich, Massachusetts.*

*Pillows*

Unlike pins and thread, the lace pillows of Ipswich were handmade locally from supplies readily available. They demonstrate the conservative use of materials to make a tool designed for heavy commercial production. Pillows used during the Colonial Revival or in later years for hobby purposes contain a wide range of more elaborate and costly materials. Each "hobby pillow" typically bears the distinctive hallmarks of its maker and shows evidence of great care taken to make it look "pretty." The pillows are available in a wide variety of shapes and sizes that are more suited to the personal taste of the hobby lace maker than to heavy practical use, and they are often embellished with personal markings, embroidery, or even mementos. By contrast, the Ipswich pillow was plain, simple, sturdy, and utilitarian, affirming its use in an industry.

The study of a lace pillow (see fig. 17) is a complex undertaking because there can be so many components in just one pillow, such as lace, pins, thread, bobbins, the pricking, the outer layer of fabric, the inner layer of fabric, and the core of filling material. In addition, a pillow might have other attachments, such as a small pocket to hold the lace as it is produced, articles hidden in the side openings, or a pincushion.

The outer layer of fabric is a cover, its task being to provide a clean work surface. It is changed periodically to keep the lace and working surface clean. The inner layer of fabric is part of the structure of the pillow itself. Building a pillow of the type used in Ipswich starts with this inner layer of fabric, which is sewn into a tube shape, with one end gathered together and tied off. The tube is then very tightly packed with the filling material, and the open end is gathered into place and secured.

The origins of lace pillows are certain. They are shaped in a traditional English bolster style, such as in fig. 17. Ipswich pillows are most often filled with saltwater grasses from the Ipswich marshes. "Salt hay" was a thriving staple in Ipswich from the earliest settlements, which used the salt marsh grasses to make thatched roofs for homes and bedding for animals. While many materials, including hay, straw, wood shavings, sand, human hair, and modern-day foam products have been used to fill lace pillows, saltwater grasses have traditionally made the best pillows. Sand makes a heavy pillow and has a tendency to shift, leaving areas on the pillow's surface that cannot hold the pins securely. They are also prone to shedding grit, making them less than desirable. Wood shavings have an annoying characteristic in that they are apt to shed tiny splinters. By contrast, the dried salt-marsh grasses are very fine and allow for a compact pillow that firmly holds the pins in place without shedding splinters or grit or being too heavy. These pillows have a long tradition of durability, with the added benefit that the salt content of the grasses discourages bug infestation, a real problem in the eighteenth century.

These bolster-style pillows were made in a cylinder, with the fabric gathered down on either end, leaving an opening at both ends. These openings (see fig. 18) have allowed the study of the contents of the pillows without causing any damage. Many lace makers seemed to have used these spaces as a place to secrete away small items. These nooks have been a source of curiosity as they have yielded many amusing finds, such as herbs, poems, newspaper articles, lace, prickings, paper orange and candy wrappers, and a tally of finished lace, insightful tokens of everyday living from another time. Herbs were used to discourage bugs, and they provided a pleasant scent as the pillow was turned. Poems and newspaper items articulate the inspirations and concerns of the individual lace maker. In one case, a newspaper clipping was valued more for its blank space than its text. It had been used to keep a tally of how much lace had been produced.

*Fig. 18.* Opening in the side of one of the Ipswich lace pillows shows the salt-marsh grass clearly, and close inspection shows the inner layer of homespun linen fabric. *Courtesy, Ipswich Historical Society, Ipswich, Massachusetts.*

*Fig. 19.* "Good ol' New England Homespun": this Ipswich lace pillow is missing its outer cover, which exposes the homespun linen fabric used in many of the Ipswich pillows. *Courtesy, Ipswich Historical Society, Ipswich, Massachusetts.*

The inner layer of fabric, as seen in fig. 19, is known as New England homespun, a coarse hand-woven fabric made from hand-spun linen thread. This was a staple made by the spinners and weavers of Ipswich. The original outer layer of fabric of the lace pillows was most often either knit stocking or cotton calico. The stocking covers (see fig. 20) commonly appear to be frame-knitted, in either a mottled blue, blue and white, or plain white, usually well worn and patched together. Notice the seams in the cover of the pillow in fig. 20; this indicates that old stockings were sewn together and reused for this purpose. Some of the pillows have an outer covering of imported calico, most likely constructed from fabric remnants of previously made dresses.

The fabrics used on the pillows are an interesting study in themselves. Some of the pillows have had new fabrics or covers added to them over the years as family members used their grandmothers' pillows during the Colonial Revival period in the early twentieth century. During this period, lace making had a revival of its own, not as an industry but as a hobby. In Ipswich, ladies interested in making lace used the old lace pillows out of a sense of nostalgia. Such pillows are interesting but offer a number of challenges to research. Some have layers from different eras, such as a pricking and lace made in the 1930s, a fabric cover from 1902, and an inner layer and filling from 1790. Research on such pillows is similar to deciphering a period home that has undergone numerous renovations.

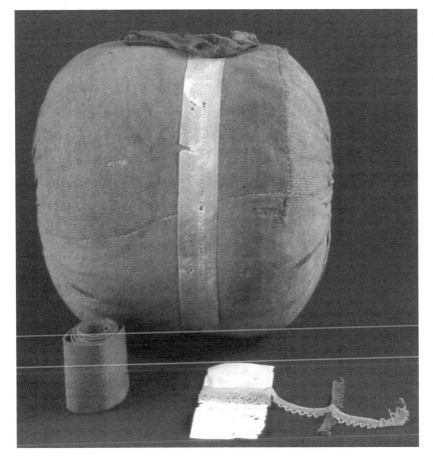

*Fig. 20.* In this Ipswich lace pillow with a blue frame knit cover, the lace on this pillow matches the lace in Mrs. Storrs's cap (see fig. 72) and the lace on a woman's cap in figs. 34 and 35. *Courtesy, Ipswich Historical Society, Ipswich, Massachusetts.*

Much work had to be done to decode the layers of history for the sake of accuracy. The approximate date of these layers developed from a study of the life dates of their owners, intensive study of each layer of materials, fiber analysis, and any accompanying documentation. Dating these items was difficult because there is no accurate method of dating textiles such as these, but scientific studies added a great deal of vital information. For example, lace made of cotton could not have been made in the eighteenth century because cotton thread suitable for lace making was not available in America until the 1820s; the type of cordlike thread made with three tiny two-ply threads wasn't invented until 1865; some fabrics were a staple in Ipswich during the late eighteenth century, and others were not available until the early twentieth century. Fiber analysis has helped date not only the threads the laces were made from but also some of the prickings and pillows.[12] These studies have helped distinguish between a pillow that has been left untouched since its use in the industry and one that has been altered over time. This type of research helps avoid errors made from misidentification of the artifacts.

*Prickings*

A pricking is a strip of material upon which a number of holes have been pricked out in a pattern. This pattern is much like a template, with each hole representing a stitch where a pin will be placed as the lace is worked. In Ipswich, prickings were made from either parchment or pasteboard, as seen in fig. 21 and as described in Joseph Dana's letter to George Cabot, July 26, 1790.

Again the concern for conservation of materials is evident in these prickings. They were overused, they often contained more than one pattern on a single pricking, yet the materials themselves were readily available and inexpensive. The prickings used in the industry were well worn (see fig. 22). The standard practice in lace making is to keep one pricking pristine, never using it to make lace. This master pricking's sole purpose is to be a template from which to create other prickings. Contrary to this standard practice, Ipswich used worn-out prickings to create new ones. This led to multiplication of mistakes and magnification of discrepancies. Lines lost their straight edge, and grids lost their symmetry.

The pricking in fig. 22 shows a fairly common practice in which two patterns are pricked out side by side with each other on the same parch-

*Fig. 21.* Set of prickings used in the Ipswich lace industry: pricking *(a)* in the background is pasteboard made of linen sometime before 1800; pricking *(b)* is made of parchment. Also seen are bobbins *(c)* and a pricker *(d)* in the foreground, used to make the holes in the prickings. *Courtesy, Ipswich Historical Society, Ipswich, Massachusetts.*

ment. This allowed for two distinctly different patterns to be contained in one strip of parchment.

## Pasteboard

Pasteboard prickings like the one in fig. 21 were handmade from 100 percent linen fibers and are therefore dated to 1800 or earlier. The analysis by the paper conservation experts at the Library of Congress shows that the prickings from Ipswich were genuine pasteboard typical of the period. Analysis also verified that the pasteboard was produced not with rags but with pure linen fibers. After 1800, pasteboard was made with rags; under a microscope, the combination of silk, cotton, and linen fibers mingled with minute specks of dye is visible. The type of pasteboard used for Ipswich prickings would have been readily available there before 1800. According to local records, pasteboard was sold at a cost of 10 shillings, 8 pence.[13]

## Parchment

Ipswich prickings were also made from parchment (see fig. 21). *Parchment* needs to be defined because it means different things to different people.

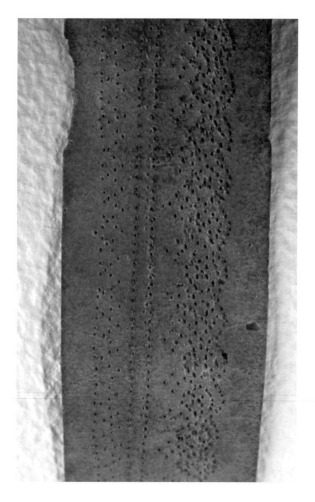

*Fig. 22.* Two patterns on one well-worn pricking, matching the lace in fig. 28. Parchment, ca. 1795–1820. *Courtesy, Ipswich Historical Society, Ipswich, Massachusetts.*

To some, it means a type of paper. To many lace makers the term refers to a pricking specifically made from the tanned hides of sheep. To a paper conservation expert it refers to an animal skin of any variety prepared in such a way that it can be written on. The word *parchment* in this text is used in the last sense.

The Ipswich prickings were made of a wide variety of tanned skins. Most of the hides were goat, sheep, and calf. Some of the more unusual ones appear to be deer or even oxen. Both pasteboard and parchment of the type used in these prickings are the stock-in-trade of bookbinders. Close examination of the skins' follicle patterns in these parchment prickings show that the pieces were from the outer edges of the hides. This telling trait implies that lace makers used the scraps left over from bookbinding for their prickings. There were many bookbinders and tanners in Ipswich and the surrounding area, such as Danvers. Samuel Fowler Jr.

(1776–1859) was a noted tanner in Danvers whose father had lived in Ipswich.[14] Ipswich had its own tanners from as early as 1634. In 1832 one establishment tanned ten thousand hides a year, paying each man a wage of one dollar and twenty-five cents a day.[15]

Pasteboard was used in 3½-inch strips long enough to go around the pillow like a belt, with the ends just meeting. Parchment prickings were, on average, 2-inch strips that encircled the pillows.

A study of remaining laces and prickings has demonstrated a curious point of interest. Matching the laces with the prickings from which they were made has shown that the narrow white laces were made on the parchment prickings and the wider black laces were typically made on the pasteboard prickings. This must have been an issue of either economy or availability. Either the narrow strips of parchment and wider strips of pasteboard happened to be readily available and perfectly suited to the work, or pasteboard was an economical or necessary alternative to parchment when a wider band was required.

Determining which pricking was used for the black laces and which for white was quite simple. The prickings used for the black laces all have the remnants of black dye embedded in the pinholes of the pricking, and often the black dye bled into the working surface of the pricking as well.

*Bobbins*

Lace-making bobbins hold the thread as it is woven into lace. The bobbins have traditionally been made of many materials including bone, wood, and even glass. They are usually adorned and richly carved and were often given as tokens of affection. Thus, lace pillows with their bobbins are sometimes a telling illustration of the life and times of their owners. Each bobbin recalled a special event or time in the lace maker's life. Bobbins have been embellished with creative abandon, some have held an infant's ring, a button from a wedding gown, the imprint of a comforting word, or a sweet note from a lover.

All bobbins are designed to do two things: hold the thread neatly in place until it is ready for use and put tension on the threads by the measure of its weight. English bobbins are noted for the beauty of their ornamentation with spangles. Spangles or beads have the function of adding weight to the bobbin. How much weight is needed depends on the fineness of the thread; heavier thread requires a heavier bobbin. The spangles also keep the bobbins from rolling.

*Fig. 23.* Four Ipswich bobbins, 4.5 inches, hollow, *Arundinaria gigantea. Courtesy, Ipswich Historical Society, Ipswich, Massachusetts.*

*Fig. 24.* Close-up of Ipswich bobbin, 4.5 inches, hollow, *Arundinaria gigantea. Courtesy, Ipswich Historical Society, Massachusetts.*

Ipswich bobbins are different: they are simple, unadorned, and functional, and they are made from an array of materials. (See figs. 23 and 24.) They are often hollow, which led to the assumption of the early 1900s that the bobbins of Ipswich were made of Chinese bamboo. Studies by experts in botany indicate that the materials used in the making these bobbins all appear to be indigenous to eighteenth-century New England or North America.

Five different materials were used to make Ipswich bobbins: A solid reed known as Bullrush, or *Scirpus maritimus*, which grew in New England in boggy water such as the saltwater marshes of Ipswich; a cork-filled reed known as *Phragmities australis*, which grew in New England; a hollow reed, *Arundinaria gigantea*, the only one of the ten thousand known species of bamboo that is native to American soil. The other two materials appear to be willow and walnut woods.

Notice that Ipswich bobbins are not lovingly carved heirlooms (see fig.

23); these are industrial bobbins. With the exception of occasional initials, these bobbins carry no marks other than the quick carving marks left by their makers (see fig. 24). Their round, slim shape makes them very fast to work with.

The study of thousands of these bobbins revealed their industrial purpose and composition, but more information was to be found in the kits of individual lace makers. Individually owned lace kits that have remained undisturbed since the time of the industry are rare. One such kit can be seen in fig. 25. Notice the bobbins that are a part of this kit.

## A Puzzling Question

The study of the bobbins collected over the years from many different lace makers and kept in bulk has yielded some very interesting information. Certainly, these bulk bobbins were made of the same five varieties of wood and reed described earlier. However, what is even more interesting

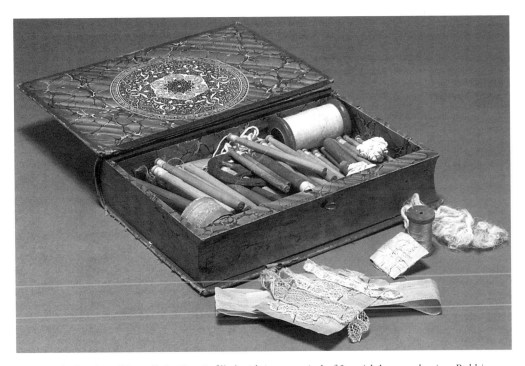

*Fig. 25.* The lace kit of Priscilla L. Gray is filled with items typical of Ipswich lace production. Bobbins are the classic assortment that came into use in the 1790s. The lavendar card holds samples of lace, and the back of the card reads: "Lace of the kind made in Ipswich, Massachusetts stemming from Buckinghamshire, Eng." *Priscilla Gray Lace Kit—photograph by Jeffrey Kykes—123910. Photograph courtesy Peabody Essex Museum.*

is the fact that these bobbins had all been carved by the same method, using exactly the same techniques regardless of the materials from which they were made. The similarity is so striking that it looks as if they were all carved by just a few people and over a short period of time. What happened to cause this?

To answer this question the bulk bobbins were compared to the bundles of bobbins from individual kits, such a Priscilla Gray's kit in fig. 25. One would logically expect that, since each lace maker worked independently, each lace maker would therefore have a set of bobbins that were a little different from the others, depending on who made her bobbins and what materials were readily available. Would some kits contain bobbins of the wooden type, while others might have only the reed type, or only the American bamboo type?

### A Discovery

The bobbins and kits from before and after the industry do show this expected variety. The original expectation that bobbins from the height of the industry would also show this variety proved wrong. What has been discovered is that the kits used during the height of the industry are identical to each other. Each kits contains an identical set of bobbins that show the same carving marks and were all made from the same assortment of wood and reed materials. The bobbins in these kits are also an exact match to the bulk bobbins.

This seeming small detail is significant news. It strongly suggests that at the height of the industry the bobbins came from the same source, indicating that at some point each lace maker did not make or independently obtain her own bobbins. The bobbins had to have been made in large quantities at one central source and then distributed to the lace makers, so that all the lace makers had the same type and assortment of bobbins. This probably happened because the industry became more organized during this period. This information from the artifacts themselves demonstrates a move to the involvement of men, most likely through a commission merchant, in the industry.

It is interesting to note that the lace pillows from this period demonstrate the same characteristics. They too look as if they were all made at one central location and distributed to the lace makers. This is even more evidence in favor of the involvement of commission merchants. There are several notable men with ties to Ipswich who could have performed this function. One was John Lakeman, a merchant who plied his trade in "European, India & American Goods" at No. 74 Cornhill in Boston. The other possibility was the Heard family.

There appears to have been a stronger link between the handmade-lace industry in Ipswich and the machine-lace industry than oral tradition recalls. The opening of the machine-lace industry in 1824 was not a serendipitous event. Worth serious consideration is the fact that Joseph Dana, whose report on the lace industry became well known, and the Heard family, who were directly involved in setting up the machine-lace industry, were close neighbors. Also worth considering is the fact that the hand-run netting produced by these new machines required the skills of accomplished lace makers to finish the product into lace for the market. Where in New England could one find a lot of lace makers and an established market for the lace? Ipswich, of course! It has been shown that many of the women who worked in the handmade-lace industry became involved in the machine-lace company. While no documentation has been discovered to date that fully articulates what exactly happened between these two industries, these factors lead one to suspect that the Heard family saw the potential for profits from Joseph Dana's report and became involved in the organization of the handmade-lace industry and then later introduced the machine-lace industry with the documented help of associates. During this same period local account books are void of lace transactions, whereas lace transactions in Boston merchants' account books are vigorous. This too would be consistent with the involvement of a commission merchant. The lace could have been marketed directly into the mainstream networks in Boston. Once men were involved in the industry, it became more organized, and the evolution to machine laces became inevitable.

It seems that each artifact, no matter how simple, has its own story to tell. The bobbins held one last, rather charming surprise. The technique used to work with this type of bobbin is called throwing. In the hands of an experienced lace maker the bobbins move back and forth very rapidly and produce a rhythmic sound. In working with these bobbins it was discovered that the Ipswich bobbins make a sound much like wood chimes—a rather pleasant discovery.

*Other Tools*

There are other items associated with the industry, such as prickers, baskets, and "horses." The pricker is a small tool used to prick out the pattern of holes on a parchment pricking (see fig. 22). Two of these prickers from the industry are still in existence at the Whipple House in Ipswich, Massachusetts.

Many of the Ipswich pillows are associated with baskets. This has caused much speculation and variation of opinion as to whether the basket was used to hold a pillow to keep it from rolling when it was not in use or was used with the pillow while the lace was being made. There is no documentation that can confirm how or even if these baskets were used in the industry. What can be said is that basket making was a part of Ipswich as early as 1639, when Thomas Bridan, a basket maker, was granted six acres of land "to plant osers."[16]

The lace horse is a three-legged structure much like the four-legged carpenters' horse that is used to saw wood. In the case of lace making, the horse is used to keep lace pillows securely in place on the lap. The collections of the Whipple House contain a curiously large number of these horses. They suffer the same fate as the baskets in that they lack documentation as to their origin. They appear to be rather short for a carpenter's horse and do not have the saw marks expected from use in woodworking. They are of the appropriate height for a lace horse. But were they really part of the industry or something constructed for a demonstration during the Colonial Revival or later? Perhaps future research will provide more answers.

The tools of the lace maker are intriguing not only for their simplicity but also because they are such personal items. More than two thousand bobbins from the industry had been discovered at the time of this writing, handmade bobbins that are over two hundred years old. Unlike the cold, hard edges of a piece of machinery, each bobbin has known the warmth of the hands of an Ipswich lace maker. Each piece of lace began in a busy early American home. Each pricking witnessed the crossing and twisting of each thread, frustration over stopping to repair a broken thread, and the intense gaze and touch of a woman working to bring comfort to her family.

2. TOOLS OF THE TRADE

1. Joseph Dana to George Cabot, July 26, 1790, Alexander Hamilton Papers, Manuscript Department, Library of Congress, Washington, D.C. (hereafter Hamilton Papers).

2. Abigail Adams to John Adams, July 16, 1775, in Natalie S. Bober, *Abigail Adams, Witness to a Revolution* (New York: Aladdin Paperbacks, 1995), page 56.

3. Pat Earnshaw, *A Dictionary of Lace* (Shire Publications, 1982), p. 124.

4. Judith Reiter Weissman and Wendy Lavitt, *Labors of Love: America's Textiles and Needlework, 1650–1930* (Wings Books, 1994), p. 172

5. "Thread lace" was a popular term for lace made from linen thread. This term distinguished lace made from linen thread from that made of silk or the metallic threads of gold or silver.

6. Pat Earnshaw, *Threads of Lace, from Source to Sink* (Guildford, UK: Gorse Publications, 1989), p. 24.

7. For more information on fibers, see Earnshaw, *Threads of Lace*.

8. Pat Earnshaw, *Threads of Lace*, pg 24.

9. Ibid.

10. John Leander Bishop, *A History of American Manufactures, from 1608 to 1860* (London: Samson Low, Son & Co., 1868), p. 362.

11. "Silkworms," *Queen* 40 (1866): 119.

12. Fiber and materials analysis of the prickings and lace samples enclosed with Joseph Dana's letter were done by the paper conservation office of the Library of Congress, Washington, D.C. All other fiber analysis was done by the textile department of the Smithsonian Institute's National Museum of American History, Washington, D.C.

13. Account Book of Timothy Brag of Ipswich, July 28, 1768, Ipswich Historical Society, Ipswich Mass., account of Dame Brown, wife to John, pasteboard sold at 0.10.8.

14. Harriet Silvester Tapley, *Chronicles of Danvers (Old Salem village), Massachusetts, 1632–1923* (Danvers, Mass.: Danvers Historical Society, 1923), p. 118.

15. Joseph B. Felt, *History of Ipswich, Essex, and Hamilton* (Cambridge, Mass., 1834; reprint, Ipswich, Mass.: Clamshell Press, 1966), p. 96.

16. Ibid., p. 96. For more information on New England baskets, see Robert Frost, "New England Baskets," *Antiques Magazine* (August 1998): 174–81.

*Silk and thread lace, of an elegant texture, are manufactured here by women and children.*
—Jedidiah Morse, *The American Gazetteer*

THE TEXTILE CURATORS' WORK is complicated by the fact that lace comes in an enormous variety of colors, styles, types, materials, regions, and patterns. For this reason the identification of lace represents an in-depth specialty of its own. Laces have been made for centuries in many different locations throughout the world. Each region borrowed from others while developing laces unique to its own location, and the differences among the laces can be dramatic or extremely subtle. Add to this the relocation of lace makers from one country to another; the Colonial Revival period in the United States, when lace making regained some popularity; and modern-day lace makers who travel the world to learn techniques from many different lace-making regions. Identifying a single piece of lace without any documentation is a challenging task.

*Understanding Lace*

To make lace a little more understandable it helps to begin with a knowledge of the methods of making lace. The first step to identifying lace is to determine whether the piece was handmade or machine-made. The focus of this study will remain within the category of handmade lace, which includes the following styles: knitted, crocheted, knotted, hairpin, tatted, needle, and bobbin lace. Ipswich lace was a handmade bobbin lace, meaning it was made with tools such as a lace pillow, a pricking, pins, and threads wound on bobbins, as seen in fig. 26.

The technique of bobbin lace making is much like weaving in miniature. Instead of a warp there are passive threads, and instead of a weft there are working threads. Instead of a loom there is a system of pins to hold the threads in place on a pricking until the work is complete and the tension is set.

Bobbin lace can be a continuous or straight lace, or it can be noncontinuous lace, which means that design elements or motifs are individually

*Fig. 26.* Ipswich lace pillow in basket with lace made of cotton. The pillow has a new cover, ca. 1930s; the deeper layers of the pillow are ca. 1800. *Courtesy, Ipswich Historical Society, Ipswich, Massachusetts.*

made, one at a time.[1] With individual motifs, the design elements, such as flowers, leaves, and scrolls, are individually made using bobbins; then the background netting, or groundwork, and fillings are added, and the individual pieces are in a sense "sewn" together to form the whole piece or length of lace. Honiton is an English lace of this type. Straight lace, on the other hand, varies from Honiton in that the fillings, design elements, and grounds are all worked as one continuous fabric. In these laces a single thread under magnification can often be followed through the entire piece, from the straight or sewing edge into the groundwork, then into the design elements to the picot edge, and finally back into the body of the lace. Ipswich lace is a bobbin lace of this type. Some of the other types of straight laces are Bucks Point, Lille, Chantilly, Mechlin, and Torchon. Not surprisingly, Ipswich shares some characteristics with these types of lace.

Knowing that Ipswich lace is a handmade bobbin lace of the straight or continuous type is the foundation on which one begins to understand this appealing lace.

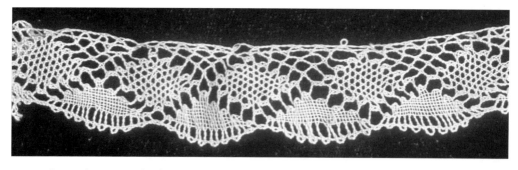

*Fig. 27.* Cotton lace reported to have been made by "Goody Caldwell." The term *goody* or *goodwife* was the proper address for a common woman in the seventeenth century. It would have been outdated by the time of Mrs. Thomas Caldwell, born Mary Boardman in Ipswich in 1780. The term was added to the label during the Colonial Revival. *Courtesy, Ipswich Historical Society, Ipswich, Massachusetts.*

### Characteristics of Ipswich Lace

Ipswich lace has a charm of its own. It isn't one of the most elaborate or finely worked laces. It didn't develop out of one of the great and well-known lace-making regions or schools. Yet there is a home-grown spirit about the lace that is hard to miss. It is much more than a quaint oddity of the past. In many cases it has a simplicity, a kind of unassuming honesty that speaks to a time when ingenuity and hard work were survival skills. It recalls a time when busy hands were seen as a sign of virtue and integrity.

### English versus Ipswich

The puzzling qualities and idiosyncrasies of Ipswich lace mirror the period during which the industry existed. Some of the laces were a challenge to differentiate from English lace because most of the women who made lace in Ipswich had emigrated from the lace-making centers of England; once in America they made the same lace they had made in England; in addition to this, the American colonies were the single largest importer of English lace.

Therefore, a fragment of lace (such as seen in fig. 28) found in Great-grandmother's old trunk could have been made by her in England and brought with her to the colonies, it could have been made in England by someone else and imported, or it could have been made in America by someone else who emigrated from England.

Complicating the picture is the colonial revival that took hold at the turn of the century (late 1800s to early 1900s) in America. During this period "old fashion" became popular, and times long gone were recalled through a decidedly romanticized perspective. Not surprisingly, lace making became popular once again, this time returning as a hobby rather than a profession. In Ipswich it was the vogue to use your grandmother's old pillow and prickings and try to reproduce the lace she had once made during the years of the industry. Hobbyists saw lace making as a charming pastime, a view their grandmothers would not have shared. Lace making was hard, tedious work. The fast-paced repetitive work and pushing of pins were hard on the hands. Bending over a lace pillow was hard on the back. And working with such fine threads, especially the black threads, under typically poor lighting was hard on the eyes. For professional lace makers the effort was a purposeful undertaking focused on generating enough resources to buy clothing and food rather than an optional leisure-time amusement. Leisure was not a realistic part of the average eighteenth-century woman's experience. Even women of the nineteenth century who had the freedom to "call on" others or socialize were expected to keep their hands busy with some form of productive endeavor such as quilting or needlework. While it is true that, in the eighteenth century, American life had changed since earlier times, life for most women continued to be very demanding. Their duties were many and their days long.

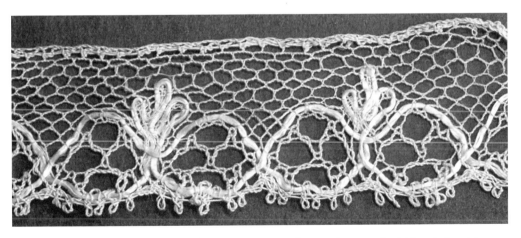

*Fig. 28.* White lace, English or Ipswich, linen, ca. 1795–1820, that matches several prickings in Ipswich, see fig. 22. *Courtesy, Ipswich Historical Society, Ipswich, Massachusetts.*

In eighteenth-century Ipswich both imported and domestically made lace was abundant for those who could afford such a luxury. Because of the fine distinctions between lace making in England versus skills learned in England and used in America, great care has been taken in identifying Ipswich lace. Fortunately, there are samples of Ipswich laces that are extremely well documented, and identification is immutable. From these well-documented specimens the characteristics of Ipswich lace have been defined, making it possible to identify with reasonable certainty other lace samples that were not so well documented. Such identification has been done with caution and great care. The laces identified through this research fall into one of several categories, as outlined below.

1. *Genuine Ipswich laces with solid provenance.* These would include such items as the samples of lace at the Library of Congress, with the accompanying letters of Joseph Dana. (See fig. 29.) This kind of documentation is obviously the ideal, but unfortunately, such discoveries are rare. However, this does not mean that our understanding stops with written documents. Like archeological artifacts, many can be identified by clues gained from the characteristics of the artifact itself and the items that accompany and surround the artifact. Careful analysis of the lace and tools has revealed a great deal about Ipswich lace, making it possible to identify pieces that are without written documentation, such as those discussed in the following categories.

2. *Genuine Ipswich laces without written provenance.* This category includes lace kits and samples of lace included in these kits from lace makers who were known to be part of the industry of lace making in Ipswich. These kits are of particular interest because they were used only by their owners and have been left undisturbed by hobbyists in later years. Except for the damage wrought by time, these kits are much as their owners left them. Such finds give a clearer understanding of what each lace maker used and what kinds of lace she made on her pillow. These kits often have lace that was in the process of being made, with bobbins still attached—bobbins that are identifiable as unique to the Ipswich lace industry.

Much as the unfinished canvas of a painter speaks volumes, the laces in the process of being made and the additional prickings found with them provide solid data on the types of lace made in Ipswich. An example of this is the lace kit of Elizabeth Lord Lakeman at the National Museum

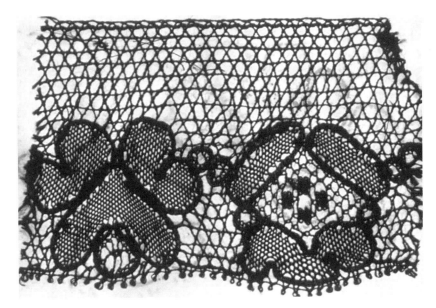

*Fig. 29.* Ipswich lace in black silk, ca. 1789–1790. The design appears to be inspired by the earlier metal laces. *Courtesy of the Library of Congress, Washington, D.C.*

of American History. Mrs. Lakeman can be placed in Ipswich during the time of the industry from vital statistics and census records. Her kit contains a fully dressed lace pillow with lace in the process of being made as well as bobbins and additional prickings. A study of her kit confirms both the type of lace made in the industry and the tools used. Each item is consistent with or identical to the types of laces seen in other kits, as well as the tools used in the Ipswich industry.

3. *Ipswich laces that can be identified by previously gathered evidence.* These laces have undergone intense scrutiny and study and have been shown to match the laces in the above categories. They have the same patterns, techniques, stitches, angles and measurements, types of mistakes, threads, and dyes as the more thoroughly documented laces. Most can be matched to the prickings from which they were made. Because imported lace did not come with its pricking, this is a very important distinction. Some of these laces have been tucked into lace pillows used during the era of the industry. Fiber analysis has been done on the existing samples of lace to help identify when each was made.

4. *Laces of the type known to have been made in Ipswich.* There are some laces among the Ipswich artifacts that are simply of the *type* known to have been made in Ipswich even when they are attached to an authentic Ipswich pillow. While these laces match the kind of lace made during the

*Fig. 30.* The lace pillow of Mrs. Low, who was born in Ipswich in 1789 (pillow ca. 1800, lace ca. 1865–1898). *Courtesy, Ipswich Historical Society, Ipswich, Massachusetts.*

industry, they also could have been made in Ipswich a time after the existence of the industry. One example of this is the lace on Mrs. Low's pillow, a classic Ipswich lace pillow used in the industry in the early years of the 1800s.

Mrs. Low was born in Ipswich in 1789. She began her involvement in the industry as a child, which is evident by the small size of her pillow. As seen in fig. 30, lace is still on the pillow. However, is it real Ipswich lace made by Mrs. Low during the time of the industry or something added later by her or someone else?

There are many clues to be examined. The pillow is authentic for the industry. The covering on the outer layer of the pillow is the stocking cover typical on other pillows used in the industry. The pricking is from the industry, it matches dozens of other prickings made of the same material with the same pattern pricked out on them, and it is from the same period. The design or pattern of the lace is one that could be considered a staple of the Ipswich industry. But is this particular piece of lace from the Ipswich industry?

The lace on Mrs. Low's pillow demonstrates a faltering level of skill, which is indicative of lace made by a very young person, a lace maker with beginning skills, or possibly an elderly person or someone with poor eyesight. (See fig. 31.) It would be tempting to take the established knowledge that Mrs. Low was very young when she was working in the industry and conclude that this must be her lace and that the discrepancies in her lace were simply a sign of her tender years. However, much more information was necessary before secure conclusions could be drawn.

Further examination of the pillow showed that the pins were poorly placed (see fig. 31). A proficient lace maker places pins in a precise and

*Fig. 31.* Close-up of lace on Mrs. Low's pillow, cotton, ca. 1865–1898. *Courtesy, Ipswich Historical Society, Ipswich, Massachusetts.*

uniform way. Beginning lace makers tend to place them in a more haphazard or crooked fashion, giving the appearance of a picket fence in need of repair. Mrs. Low's pillow has this malady. Even more telling, the pins themselves are not of the type available in the late eighteenth and early nineteenth centuries—that is, they are not the handmade type but appear to be one-piece machine-made pins, which dates them after the 1830s. Therefore, the lace had to have been made after the 1830s. These factors fostered more questions and suspicions about its date.

To answer these questions a small sampling of thread from the lace was taken to the Smithsonian's National Museum of American History for fiber analysis. A study by fiber experts resulted in two important discoveries. The first was that the thread used to make this piece of lace was cotton. As we have seen, cotton thread was not used in handmade lace until after the 1820s, and the type of pin used dates Mrs. Low's lace to sometime after the 1830s.

The second and more interesting piece of information produced by the fiber analysis was the structure of the thread itself. According to the experts at the museum, the lace is made from a very distinctive, tiny six-strand cord made up of three two-ply threads (see fig. 32). This is of importance because that type of thread was not invented until 1865. Therefore, the lace on the pillow must have been made after 1865, which is consistent with the type of pins on the pillow and the use of cotton. The pillow was donated to the Ipswich Historical Society in 1898 and was put

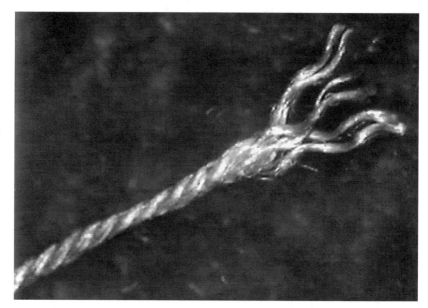

*Fig. 32.* The thread used to make the lace on Mrs. Low's pillow is cotton cord of three two-ply strands, ca. 1865–1898. *Fiber analysis and photograph courtesy of the National Museum of American History; fibers courtesy, Ipswich Historical Society, Ipswich, Massachusetts.*

on display. Putting all this information together dates the lace sometime after 1865 and before 1898.

The only remaining question was, who made the lace? By 1865, Mrs. Low was about seventy-six years of age. Elizabeth Lord Lakeman, another lace maker, made lace on her pillow until she was in her nineties, and it is possible that Mrs. Low made lace in her later years too. Or the lace could have been made during the Colonial Revival period by a hobbyist or perhaps a descendant of Mrs. Low. To draw a final conclusion, a deeper look at the lace was necessary.

There can be many reasons for poorly worked lace: working too fast, being very young or inexperienced, failing eyesight, or hands that are not as agile as they once were. Each of these factors produces a slightly different type of problem. The lace on Mrs. Low's pillow does not look as though it was made by a skilled lace maker advanced in years. The mistakes in the lace look more like those that might be generated by lack of skill or by a beginner to lace making. Mrs. Low was very young during the industry period, and it is possible that her lace-making skills had not advanced beyond her childhood levels before she was drawn on to other things. Certainly, she could have tried to pick up her pillow again in her later years.

However, while it is still conceivable that Mrs. Low made the lace on this pillow, it is unlikely. It is more plausible that the lace on this pillow was made during the Colonial Revival period by a hobbyist with limited skill, perhaps a descendant, who was trying to copy the lace made by Mrs. Low.

This theory makes sense in the context that the pillow was given to the Ipswich Historical Society during the Colonial Revival. The reworking of the lace could have been done in deliberate preparation for putting the pillow on display in the Whipple House, with good intentions—to show the public what the pillow would have looked like when it was in use. Many old photographs from the early 1920s show this same pillow, unchanged from its present condition, on display in the background.

Even the handwriting on a note on the pillow is of a style consistent with the period (see fig. 33). Unless other documentation is discovered, the most defensible conclusion is that the lace is of the type made in Ipswich during the industry but not actually made during that period.

5. *Lace associated with Ipswich.* There are some laces identified with Ipswich that have an uncertain origin or lack enough direct or indirect information to confirm a connection with the lace industry. There were

*Fig. 33.* Note from Mrs. Low's pillow. *Courtesy, Ipswich Historical Society, Ipswich, Massachusetts.*

several women, most notably Carry B. Ladd and Elizabeth Newton, who took on the commendable task of collecting laces and lace artifacts from the attics of old lace-making families in Ipswich. Unfortunately, many of these fragments were without any documentation or other artifacts that would lend evidence as to the origins of the pieces. These laces have been carefully preserved, honoring oral tradition and the assumption that they were from the lace-making industry. Some of the laces in this category could have been made either in England, in America, or on a ship somewhere in between.

The lace in fig. 28 is typical of both Ipswich lace and English lace. It is made of an exceedingly fine two-ply linen thread with an *S* twist. It is diminutive compared to the lace made in similar patterns during the early 1900s. It matches another piece of lace, accompanied by a note that declares, "Ipswich lace, thread 250." This information alone does not identify the lace with Ipswich. However, there are many prickings in the Ipswich collection from the era of the industry that match this piece of lace. The fact that imported laces do not come with their prickings makes a strong case for this piece's relationship to the industry, and this connection is not refuted by the other evidence.

## The Ipswich Collection

It should be noted that the Ipswich Historical Society has a large collection of laces that has no connection with Ipswich. Many of these laces are certainly worthy of study and preservation, but they are not related to the industry.

As evidenced by the study of Mrs. Low's lace pillow, lace itself is much like a document waiting to be read. The number of twists on each thread, the patterns, the types of stitches, the way the gimp threads are attached, and even the angles of the work tell the story of the origin of the lace and much about its maker. These characteristics help identify Ipswich lace.

## The Puzzle of Ipswich Lace

Many experienced modern-day lace makers study very intensively to ensure that the lace they make is a perfect technical execution of the particular type of lace they are studying. They make sure that the thread size is just right, the tension on the threads is just right, the technique is just right, the diameter and length of the pins are just right, and most important, that each twist and crossing of threads is strictly in adherence with the rules of that particular genre of lace making. For example, if the lace maker is making Torchon lace, the angle of her ground will be worked in a grid that is at a 45-degree angle, in accordance with the guidelines for that type of lace. Lace makers today are often willing to remove hours of work to correct a single mistake. To such well-trained eyes and expectations of perfection, Ipswich lace is a challenge. It is a lace that embodies "mistakes" boldly left in place, many adapted styles and patterns, and a great deal of creative license. Such anomalies could easily lead one to dismiss the lace as inferior. However, in doing so an understanding of this uncommon industry on American soil would be lost. The variations in Ipswich lace are there for a reason worth deeper exploration.

*Commercial Lace*

The most important thing to understand about Ipswich lace is that it was a commercial lace. Today we make a distinction between "fine jewelry" and "costume jewelry." Drawing a parallel to Ipswich lace, we can say that Ipswich lace was "costume lace" rather than "fine lace," meaning that this lace was not intended be an exemplary demonstration of the finest of lacemaking methodology. Rather this product was made to be competitive in the marketplace. It was a means to an end. As one would expect, it was made as quickly as possible, it catered to the fashions of the day, and it was very reasonably priced.

Ipswich laces demonstrate many details indicative of a commercial industry: on a technical level the laces show idiosyncrasies that are the result of fast production; over time the designs were simplified to make the lace faster to work; the patterns were taken from what was popular at the time, showing a concern for turning out a competitive product; and the lace bears the marks of being made on prickings that were overused.

Lace produced on a commercial level, as in eighteenth-century textile production, was not a flawless object of art. It was a balance of practical use, fast production, and responses to fashion. Ipswich lace is an excellent example of this type of production. If speed was a significant value, the smaller anomalies in the work were ignored. Ipswich lace routinely demonstrates mistakes that are clearly visible even to the untrained eye. However, these deviations are more a testament to why and how the laces were made than a sign of deficiency. The strategy of the Ipswich lace maker made a lot of sense, especially with the black laces. Mistakes or discrepancies in black thread are much harder to see than those in the same lace made of white thread. Also, the lace was seen from a distance, not framed flat or on display for study or scrutiny. Such issues became moot when many yards of the lace were gathered into ruffles. Any imperfection quickly vanished among the folds.

This does not mean that the lace makers had no concern for quality work. There is a reference in a lecture by Sarah E. Lakeman, circa 1903 (now in the manuscript collection of the Ipswich Historical Society), in which she recalls how the lace was gathered up once a week and examined for quality. The account acknowledges that many women were quite anxious as they waited for word of whether their lace had been found acceptable, judged to be of a quality that merited being presented at market for sale. Ms. Lakeman was quoting her mother, Susan Lakeman. Concern for quality and fashion were considerable.

*Evolution in Design*

An interesting study in itself, the changes in fashion and competition in the marketplace caused an evolution in the type of lace made over time. The designs and details of the lace became both larger and more simplified, illustrating one of the clear earmarks of an industry. There are three types of Ipswich lace: very fine, detailed work with small, intricate designs; the black laces, with large, simplified designs; and a lot of Bucks Point and Torchon that is more consistent with the early nineteenth century.

*The Early Laces*

Analysis of laces dating from the 1760s shows a pattern and a deliberate trend that makes sense in the context of commercial production. These laces were made of linen and demonstrate the most intricate designs. They were made in limited quantities by individual women who conceived of the idea of selling their lace. These laces from the 1760s were usually sold, according to contemporary account books, in three- to six-yard pieces, they were valued at sixteen to eighteen shillings per yard before the dealer's markup. That would mean that a yard of lace was approximately equal in value to a cord of wood or to sixteen pounds of sheep's wool. Imagine taking six yards of lace neatly rolled up in a pocket and being able to exchange that parcel for a three-week supply of wood, enough wool for making a sweater, a bushel of rye, a jar of molasses, and some thread to make more lace. The lace was a valuable product.

*The Central Laces*

Understandably, the demand for lace grew. Along with the increased volume of production the designs became larger and the patterns simplified. Instead of tiny fans and flowers, the designs were large bold flowers worked with stitches that could be done quickly. Many of the patterns are remarkably similar to the archaic patterns of the metal laces that were used to adorn furniture and coaches. The Ipswich lace makers appear to have been looking at designs around them that they could exploit to further the lace production. The advantages of the metal lace patterns were that they were larger, simpler, and faster to work. Several lace experts have noted how the designs appear to be "watered down." This is most likely driven by the need for speedy production.

The size of thread used was not adjusted for the larger pattern, and the result, as seen in some of the black Ipswich lace, is a rather thin and meager look. On the other hand, using a thread that is too large for a pattern will result in a chunky, heavy lace. The emphasis on ease of production also can be seen in the way the gimp threads were carried through the work and in the types of stitches used in the groundwork and fillings. By the 1790s this lace with simpler designs sold for, at most, three shillings a yard.

What caused the change from lace selling at eighteen shillings per yard in the 1760s to lace selling for three shillings per yard or less in the 1790s? Since other textiles didn't experience a similar loss in value, perhaps the change in pricing over this twenty-five-year period had more to do with changes in the type of lace made and sold rather than in the devaluation of lace itself. According to advertisements, newspapers, and account books it appears that imported laces continued to be sold at higher prices. It is evident that the Ipswich industry was diligently producing a lace that would be competitively priced. Ipswich lace was either deliberately made to be more competitive and therefore more inexpensive, or the simplification of designs and quick production evolved naturally into a less expensive product. One can't help but wonder if this lower priced lace was produced deliberately, with the idea of making it more widely available and thereby allowing American women in the middle classes to wear lace.

Was the making and wearing of this lace a show of national pride and support of the American cause? Was it something more basic, like striving to be successful at market? Perhaps the lace makers simply made what sold. It would be highly speculative and wrong to assume that the Ipswich lace industry was motivated purely by politics. It is more likely that many factors played a role in the development of the industry and its success.

Ipswich lace was competitive in more ways than price. Many of the designs used in the lace were taken from what was most popular at the time and were clearly made for use in the popular black lace shawls. From accounts that remain, along with an oral tradition, Mrs. Caldwell would trade her own lace and that of other lacemakers for samples of the popular imported laces. Then she would return to Ipswich and make prickings from the new piece of lace. These would be used to produce an Ipswich version of the imported lace. The resulting product incorporated inspirations in design from other sources with the English techniques of lace making as they existed in Ipswich. The black Ipswich laces were a response to fashion and the demand for black lace.

In the early nineteenth century white lace developed a look more consistent with Bucks and Torchon lace. These laces were made from cotton in patterns that were simple to intermediate in complexity. These were the laces that the Colonial Revival focused on in the late nineteenth and early twentieth centuries. By this time it had been forgotten that Ipswich had ever made black lace. Francis Morris, in a book published in 1926, reflects on the finer laces such as the black silk lace often seen in American portraits: "There is nothing to indicate that lace of this quality could have been made anywhere in America; for such lace as was produced in the colonies, even at Ipswich—the only place known to have been a lace center of any importance—was a simple narrow edging of the Buckinghamshire type."[2] Morris bases her understanding on the white cotton laces of the last few decades of the industry and the work done by lace makers during the Colonial Revival. Joseph Dana's samples and letter apparently were not widely known when Morris was preparing her book.

Another sign of commercialism was the peculiar irregularities of lace made on prickings that were worn out. Tools from any industry bear witness to unremitting use. There is a dramatic difference between the prickings used in the industry and prickings used during the Colonial Revival period. The materials used for prickings are different; the groundwork in the industry prickings shows pinholes only in a few instances, whereas the Revival ones always have pinholes in the groundwork; and most notably, the prickings from the industry show heavy use, and the ones from the Revival show only light use. Often the prickings from the Revival period have only three or four inches used only once. This is typical of a hobby lace maker who tries a pattern briefly and then moves on to another. When a pricking is used repeatedly to produce many yards of lace, it will eventually wear out. The pinholes become enlarged, causing pin placement to be slightly off. The pins then have a tendency to lean to one side. This causes pulling on the threads that distorts the lace just slightly. When this happens, a straight line begins to waver and the lace loses its crisp even lines. In Ipswich prickings it is common to see pinholes so enlarged that two holes became one elongated hole. Ipswich lace shows characteristics consistent with overworked patterns, as expected from a commercial lace.

The signs of commercial production, as you will see, are just a few of the interesting details of this lace. Ipswich lace was made in many different patterns, widths, and materials, with variations in colors. In the world

*Fig. 34 (above).* Woman's cap with type of lace made in Ipswich, undated. *Courtesy, Ipswich Historical Society, Ipswich, Massachusetts.*

*Fig. 35 (right).* Detail of lace on woman's cap in fig. 34, with matching pricking. *Courtesy, Ipswich Historical Society, Ipswich, Massachusetts.*

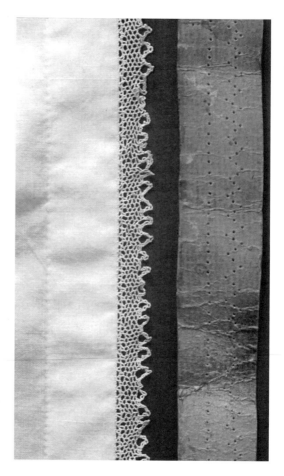

of lace production, whether a lace was made three hundred years ago or yesterday, there is a wide spectrum of differences between simple laces and those with exquisite details.

### The White Laces

The most obvious characteristic of Ipswich lace is color. Some Ipswich laces are white, and others are black; a few are blonde or a natural color. Joseph Dana refers to two categories of lace: "edgings" (see fig. 5) and "lace" (see fig. 4). From an analysis of Dana's account of the lace, the amounts made, and the corresponding values it is clear that by edgings he refers to the narrow laces, and by laces he refers to wider silk laces. The edgings were the least expensive, and the lace was the most expensive; a narrow edging is typically easier and faster to work than a piece three inches wide. With a few exceptions, white laces were typically ½ inch to 1¼ inches in width, and the black laces were usually 1¾ inches to 3 inches wide.

The white Ipswich lace is English in appearance, along the lines of Bucks Point, Downton, and Torchon. Much of the lace is small edgings that have an almost "homey" quality. Figs. 34 and 35 show one of the most commonly made edgings. This lace edges a woman's cap. In fig. 35 you can see the pricking from which the lace was made.

## The Black Laces

The black laces are typical of late-eighteenth century lace except that they appear to be unique to Ipswich. Both white and black laces demonstrate variations in levels of skill, uncorrected mistakes, tension problems, quickness of production, and techniques, even when made by the same lace maker. What makes the black laces different is design. Designs for the black laces are an interesting mix of styles. Many are watered-down or simplified images that appear to have been inspired by both English and European trends in fashion, by popular motifs of the time, and by once-popular designs of the third quarter of the eighteenth century. Some of the heavily patterned black laces are more consistent with late-eighteenth- and early-nineteenth-century metal thread laces.

The amalgamated styles of the black laces can best be attributed to the Ipswich lace makers' desire to produce a lace that would sell, and for this purpose creative license was employed, resulting in a lace unique to Ipswich. The fusion of so many different styles and patterns mas made these laces a fascinating study.

## Ipswich Lace in Detail

This section provides an in-depth study of Ipswich lace from a technical perspective. One of the most interesting discoveries in the study of Ipswich lace is the mix of English and Continental styles of lace making. The reason for this mix of style and technique has two possible answers. Some experts believe that Ipswich lace captures an earlier stage in English lace making when the influence of immigrating lace makers from the Continent was still very visible. After this period English lace developed into the classic English styles, such as Bedfordshire and Bucks, that reached maturity in the mid-nineteenth century. Ipswich lace captures this period of evolution. Other lace scholars cite the direct influence of lace makers from the Continent that could have been accepted either in England or America. In any event, Ipswich lace is an engaging amalgamation of style and technique.

## White Laces

The white Ipswich laces are easily identified with Bucks and Torchon. The groundwork demonstrates a Torchon, Bucks, or point ground or half-stitch groundwork. These laces would be familiar to modern-day lace makers, many of whom learned lace making by using these same patterns and techniques, which are indistinguishable from the lace made in England. Some patterns have been around since the late eighteenth century, and others are more typical of the nineteenth century.

## Black Laces

The black laces show an interesting metamorphosis to Ipswich Lace. Owing to the excellent conservation and protection provided by the Library of Congress, these laces are well documented and securely dated. See figs. 36 and 37 for the complete set of Ipswich lace samples that accompanied Joseph Dana's letter.

## The Neoclassical Period

The black Ipswich laces were used for the shawls that American women wore in the late eighteenth century and early nineteenth century. In *Lace: A History*, an outstanding book on the subject, Santina M. Levey expertly documents a period of lace making known as the Neoclassical Period, between 1780 and 1815, which is when the black Ipswich Laces were made. The decorative mesh grounds of the Ipswich laces are typical of these years. Levey explains that the hallmarks of this period were a "steady diminution in the importance of pattern" in tandem with the rise in popularity of lighter and softer laces. This was an important shift from the Valenciennes, Alençon, and Brussels laces that had been so popular to lighter laces, such as the blonde silk and thread laces of some of the secondary lace centers. Additionally, there was a shift in the way women dressed, clothing being simplified by the use of muslin and gauze instead

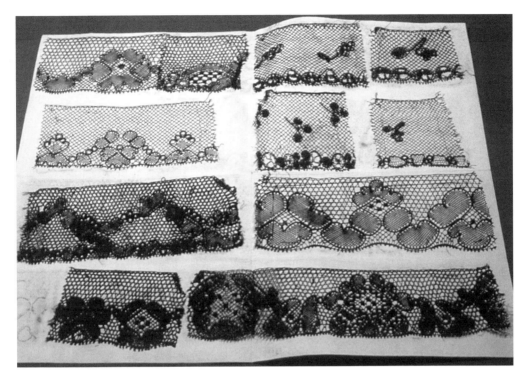

*Fig. 36.* First sheets of lace samples sent with the letters of Joseph Dana. Black silk lace, ca. 1789–1790. *Courtesy of the Library of Congress, Washington, D.C.*

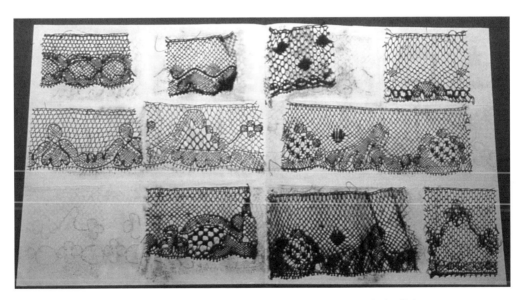

*Fig. 37.* Second sheets of lace samples sent with the letters of Joseph Dana. Black silk lace, ca. 1789–1790. *Courtesy of the Library of Congress, Washington, D.C.*

of heavy laces. The impact of these changes and the disruptions of wars played a major role in reducing the overall demands for lace,[3] as did the invention of machinery for making the lace mesh. As machine-made lace became available, the dynamics of lace, its value in the marketplace, and even the type of woman who would wear it was forever changed. During this period, as well, lace, which had been an important and prestigious accoutrement, fell out of favor as part of the "male" wardrobe.

## The Footside

The foot, footside, footing, *engrelure*,[4] or sewing edge is the straight edge on a length of lace that is intended to be sewn or attached to another fabric.[5] It is customary for English laces to be made with the footside on the right; European laces are made with the footside on the left. Pam Nottingham has noted that "it is usual to work an edging with the footside on the right."[6] This reference is to Bucks point, an English lace that is the subject of her book. Doris Southard, in a book on bobbin lace, writes: "You will find, incidentally, that all English lace makers and English books on lace making place the sewing edge or footing at the right side of the work and all European books place it on the left."[7] The black Ipswich laces, like the white laces, depart from this tradition, as all Ipswich lace appears to have been worked with the footside on the left, contrary to the English rule-of-thumb. Even the work of Elizabeth Lord Lakeman, who made lace up until her death in 1862, always made it with the foot on the left. It makes sense that she continued to make lace in the way she had learned as a girl even though women in England were working with the footside on the right by 1862.

## The Ground Work

The grounds, or mesh, of Ipswich lace is typical of the Neoclassical period. There are three types of grounds used in the black laces — Torchon, Brussels, and Point de Paris.

## Point Ground

The term *point* in lace work is a tricky one owing to the many ways in which this word is used. It can mean "stitch" in French; it can refer to an abbreviated term for needlepoint or needle laces; it can be a prefix for all

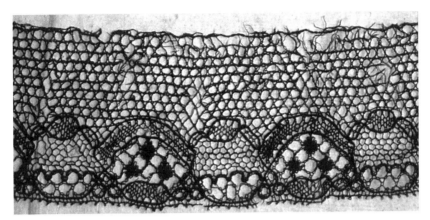

*Fig. 38.* Ipswich lace
using a point ground fill,
black silk, ca. 1785–1800.
*Courtesy, Ipswich Historical
Society, Ipswich, Massachusetts.*

lace, such as Point de Paris; and it can refer to the French origins of a type
of lace, as in the case of Bucks point. Bucks is sometimes called English
Lille, Lille being a French lace. The list is lengthy and somewhat confus-
ing. Today "point ground laces" usually refers to a type or style of lace
made by using what is known as a point ground. That is a ground like the
ones used in Chantilly or Bucks. This stitch is a cross, twist, twist, twist
(CTTT) with an uncovered pin and cross, twist, twist, twist. An exceptional study is currently underway in Europe to identify and classify all
known examples of point ground laces. While the white Ipswich laces
employ point ground as groundwork, the black laces identified to date do
not. However, the technique of point ground clearly was known to the
Ipswich lace makers and used as a filling. (See fig. 38.)

Classifications of the groundwork stitches do not come easily because
each piece of Ipswich lace contains so many variations. The three groundwork stitches listed above were identified through analysis under the cool
light of a fiberoptically lit microscope, which allows for very detailed
study, and with the expertise of Robin Lewis-Wild. Each area of groundwork was examined, and every twist and cross was counted. Even when a
lace maker strayed from a consistent pattern by working too quickly, her
intentions become obvious when an averaging of stitches is calculated.
This analysis of the details of Ipswich lace would not have been possible
without Lewis-Wild and the skills and knowledge of many other talented
lace makers.

### The Torchon/Honeycomb Ground

One of the most common grounds used in the black Ipswich laces is the
Torchon/Honeycomb. At first glance it looks very much like a variation

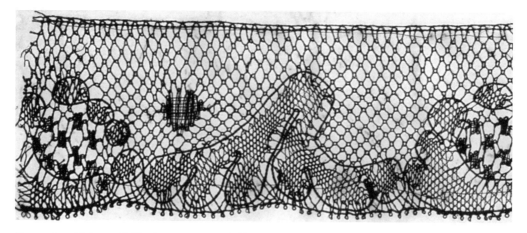

*Fig. 39.* Ipswich lace with Torchon-type ground, black silk, ca. 1789–1790. *Courtesy of the Library of Congress, Washington, D.C.*

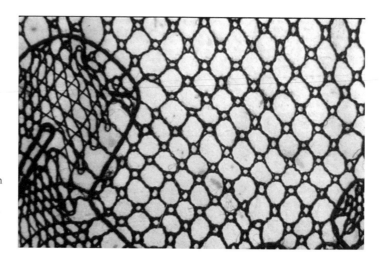

*Fig. 40.* Close-up of Ipswich lace with Torchon-type ground, black silk, ca. 1789–1790. *Courtesy of the Library of Congress, Washington, D.C.*

on a Torchon ground except that the hole left by the pin is very obvious. The reason for this is an extra twist at the pinhole. There are many names for this ground. Pat Earnshaw and Susie Johnson call it a Spanish ground.[8] Albert Von Hennenberg referred to it as double fond Torchon. Robin Lewis-Wild sees it as a variation of a Torchon ground. Carol Watson and Holly VanSciver see it as a variation of a honeycomb stitch (the honeycomb stitch used without the usual honeycomb patterned grid). Each of these experts is right. The stitch is a cross, twist, twist, pin, cross, twist, twist. It must be noted here that the number of crosses and twists varies greatly even within the same piece. Variations of two to four twists can be found between the pinhole, cross, twist, and the next stitch. The groundwork on the laces that use this ground are measured between 42 and 50 degrees. An exhaustive review of every book on lace housed at the Library of Congress leads to the conclusion that this ground was common in the eighteenth century and is seen in many laces.

## The Brussels Ground

This ground of hexagons is much like an old Mechlin ground or the Vrai Reseau or Droschel ground of Brussels lace. (See figs. 41 and 42.) Even though Brussels is a noncontinuous lace, the brides were replaced by a

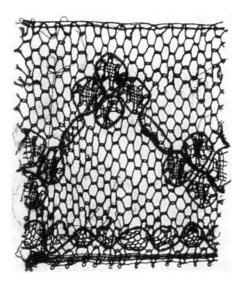

*Fig. 41.* Brussels-type ground, black silk, ca. 1789–1790. *Courtesy of the Library of Congress, Washington, D.C.*

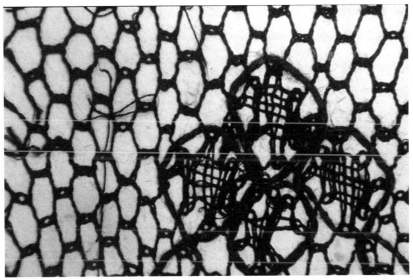

*Fig. 42.* Close-up of Ipswich lace with Brussels-type ground, black silk, ca. 1789–1790. *Courtesy of the Library of Congress, Washington, D.C.*

Dorschel ground that was in use until the mid-nineteenth century.[9] An averaged accounting of the stitches used in this ground provides a pattern of CTCT.CTCT, with one or two twists between stitches. The intended angle of the grid for this ground was likely 45 degrees. However, measurements on any individual piece of lace can vary between 45 and 55 degrees.

### The Paris Ground

Point de Paris is found in the black Ipswich laces as often as is the Torchon-style ground (see figs. 43 and 44). This ground is seen in many types of

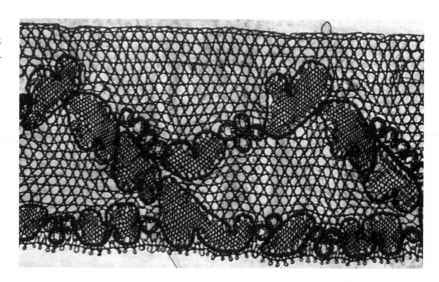

*Fig. 43.* Ipswich lace with Paris ground, black silk, ca. 1789–1790. *Courtesy of the Library of Congress, Washington, D.C.*

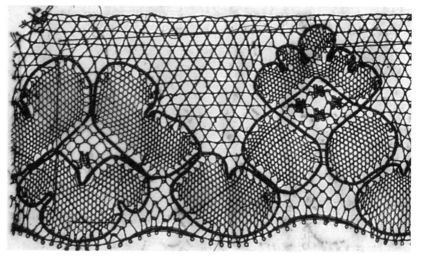

*Fig. 44.* This lace with Paris ground, one of the few examples in which pairs are carried along the header. Black silk, ca. 1789–1790. *Courtesy of the Library of Congress, Washington, D.C.*

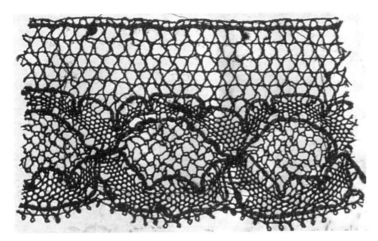

*Fig. 45.* Ipswich lace, black silk, ca. 1789–1790; the unusual texture of this lace is explained in fig. 46. *Courtesy of the Library of Congress, Washington, D.C.*

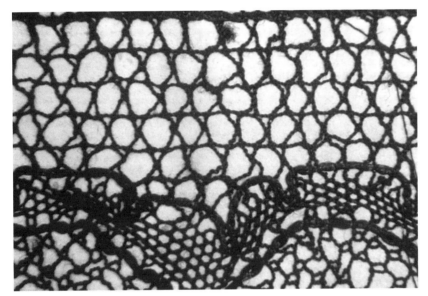

*Fig. 46.* Close-up shows an unusually high number of twists on each thread, accounting for its texture. Black silk, ca. 1789–1790. *Courtesy of the Library of Congress, Washington, D.C.*

lace contemporary with Ipswich lace, including the black Bucks point. Other names for this stitch are Fond Chant, Wire, or Kat stitch. In Ipswich laces this ground can vary any where from 60 to 68 degrees.

The look of a particular piece of lace has a great deal to do with the way the stitches are worked. Counting the number of twists and crosses of pairs of threads seems like a tedious task, but the information gathered merits such efforts. Fig. 45 is a fine example of how the number of twists can change the appearance of a piece of lace. This particular piece was a puzzle until it was examined under a microscope. The rather stunning number of twists of each pair of threads accounts for the lace's strange appearance (see fig. 46). The lace maker who worked this piece seemingly had the philosophy that if one twist was good, surely seven were better! This lace is so tightly twisted, especially in the fills, that the stitches want to turn back on themselves.

The Measurements

Bobbin-lace grounds are worked from a diagonal line from the footside. The angle of the measurements between this diagonal or working line and the straight edge of the foot helps to identify lace. For example, Torchon lace is worked on a 45-degree angle. Bucks Point is worked ideally on a 60-degree angle. In her book on the techniques of Bucks Point,[10] Pam Nottingham has a clear illustration of how a change in the angle of a grid can alter the shape of the design elements. The technique of measuring angles is of limited use with Ipswich lace because the grounds rarely conform to a consistent grid and the design elements, unlike modern lace patterns, never conform to a nice, neat grid within the same measurable angles. In modern lace patterns the design elements conform to the grid and are consistent with the rest of the lace.

In Ipswich lace the design elements are drawn first, and the grounds are added separately. The end result is that on one piece of lace there can be a number of different angles. These shifts in angles can easily be seen within one section of ground (see fig. 47). Distortions also are visible on the prickings. For this reason, measuring angles has been challenging.

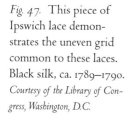

*Fig. 47.* This piece of Ipswich lace demonstrates the uneven grid common to these laces. Black silk, ca. 1789–1790. *Courtesy of the Library of Congress, Washington, D.C.*

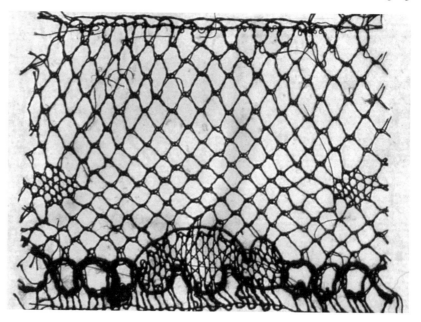

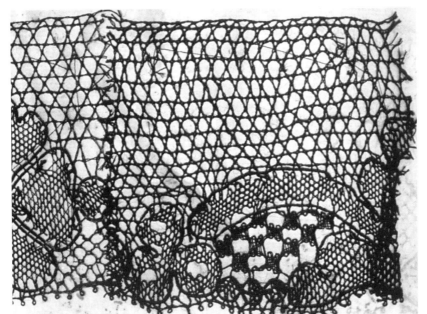

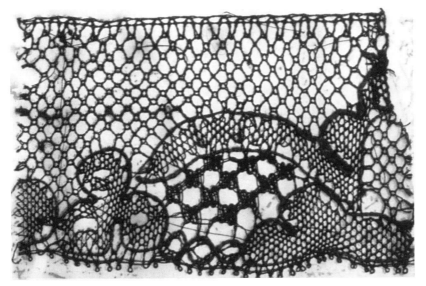

Susie Johnson and Carol Watson have done excellent work in measuring the grounds and identifying the types of stitches used in the grounds of the samples at the Library of Congress.

Today we think of the groundwork as part of the whole. Ipswich lace shows the ground as a separate entity. Figs. 48 and 49 demonstrate how a design element was placed in a pricking and the groundwork was added to the design. In this case the designs were exactly the same for both

*Fig. 50.* Half-stitch fills show the even tension and technique typical of a skilled lace maker. Black silk, ca. 1789–1790. *Courtesy of the Library of Congress, Washington, D.C.*

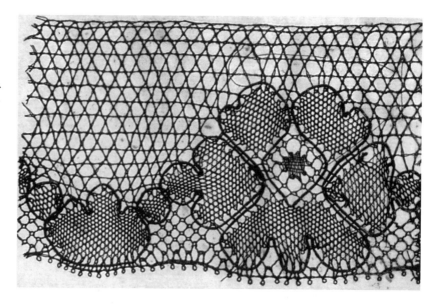

*Fig. 51.* These half-stitch fills, with uneven tension and technique, are evidence of a less skilled lace maker. Black silk, ca. 1789–1790. *Courtesy of the Library of Congress, Washington, D.C.*

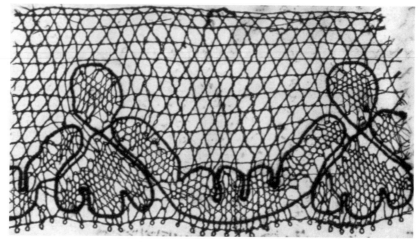

pieces, but each lace maker employed a different type of ground. In fig. 48 the ground is Point de Paris, and in fig. 49 the ground is the Torchon type.

*The Fillings and Decorative Elements*

A fill is the kind of stitch used to fill in a design element, such as a triangle, a petal, or a free-form design. These stitches can produce an effect of light or density similar to the shades of color used by a painter. The type of stitch used to fill in an area plays an important role in the appearance of the finished piece. Chantilly lace is a beautiful illustration of the effects of light and shadow that can be achieved with variations of whole and half stitches.

## The Half Stitch

The most common fill stitch in the black laces is the half stitch (see figs. 50 and 51). In Ipswich lace this filling technique is pretty straightforward. It lacks the delicate expressions of Chantilly and the exceptional lights and shadows crafted by the cloth stitch and half stitch in the Bayeux and Caen laces of the nineteenth century. In figs. 50 and 51, variations in the skills of each lace maker are pronounced.

## The Cloth Stitch

Cloth stitch is occasionally used in small amounts in some examples of the black Ipswich laces. (See fig. 52.)

## The Point Ground Fill

Like fig. 38, fig. 53 shows an example of point ground used as a fill. What by today's standards would be considered groundwork as a fill was a common

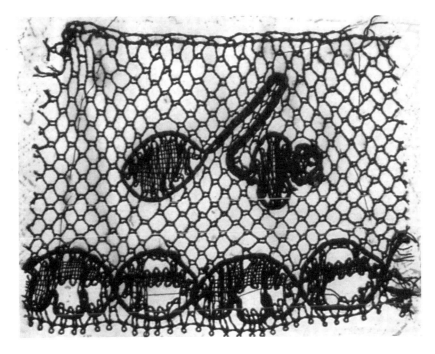

*Fig. 52.* This piece with a cloth-stitch fill matches a pricking in Ipswich and the lace on a woman's cape at the Museum of Fine Arts, Boston (see figs. 76 and 77). Black silk, ca. 1789–1790. *Courtesy of the Library of Congress, Washington, D.C.*

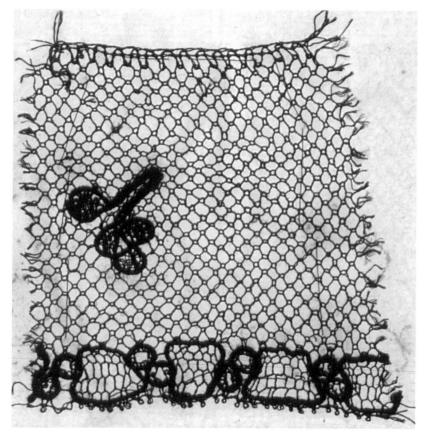

practice in Ipswich laces. This piece is very typical of Ipswich lace (see fig. 53). Notice that the groundwork, of the Torchon type, does not conform to a neat and even grid. The gimp is simple and the details few.

### The Mock Tally

Some of the fills have the appearance of a tally but are much faster and easier to work (see fig. 44). They are little squares of cloth stitch that are made with the aid of pins, unlike the technique for true tallies. This decorative technique is commonly used on many laces, including a piece of Ipswich lace found on a a shawl owned by Martha Washington.

### The Old Mayflower

This very English stitch is commonly seen in Ipswich laces. Fig. 54, which demonstrates the technique, is a detail from the piece shown in fig. 38, in which a number of fills are employed on the same piece.

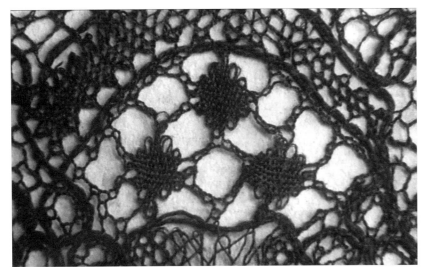

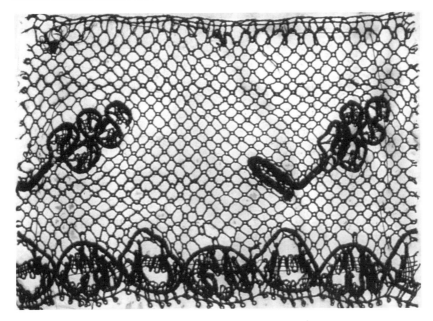

*Design Elements*

The designs used in Ipswich lace are of a wide variety. The following takes
a closer look at some of the most frequently used elements.

Free-Form Designs

Many Ipswich lace designs contain shapes that are hard to define. They
may look like beans, ladybugs, the paper dolls of childhood cut from

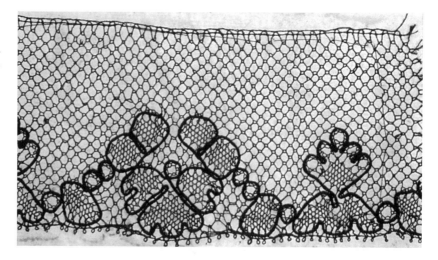

*Fig. 56.* A pansy design with many open peas, black silk, ca. 1789–1790. *Courtesy of the Library of Congress, Washington, D.C.*

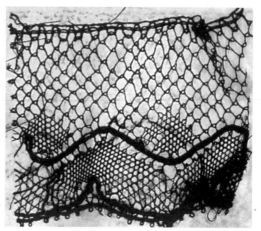

*Fig. 57.* A geometric design in black silk, ca. 1789–1790. *Courtesy of the Library of Congress, Washington, D.C.*

folded paper, or waves. As in looking at clouds, it is easy to read into these elements a multitude of images. Where the images originally came from is yet to be discovered. What can be said about these curious shapes is that they are very commonly used, especially in the silk laces. They can be seen in other laces contemporary to Ipswich lace, and it is known that Ipswich lace makers borrowed heavily from other sources.

Open Peas

The open pea is seen in fig. 56. This sample of black lace shows a pansy design with half-stitch fills embellished with open peas. The "Ipswich pea" is very much like the Bucks six-pinhole except that the Ipswich version employs both a six-pinhole and a small four-pinhole pea.

Floral/Geometric

The black laces show the most variations in designs. Much like Bucks Point, there are both floral and geometric styles of the same lace. Some designs are clearly floral in inspiration, such as the piece in figs. 44, 50, and 56. Some are more geometric, as seen in fig. 57. In this piece the header design is wavelike, with diamond shapes within the valleys of each wave.

*The Gimp*

All the black laces have gimps. Some designs use a small amount of gimp and are simple, as seen in fig. 57. And some have an impressive amount of gimp, which richly embellishes the design (fig. 59). In some samples the gimp runs continuously through the the piece, and in others it is started and stopped as needed for the individual elements as in fig. 58.

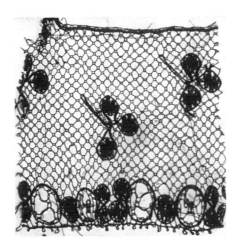

*Fig. 58.* Demonstration of the simple use of a noncontinuous gimp. Black silk, ca. 1789–1790. *Courtesy of the Library of Congress, Washington, D.C.*

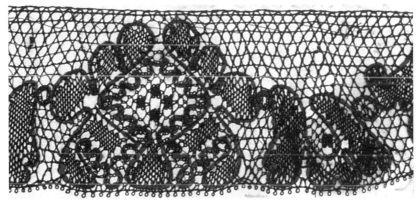

*Fig. 59.* This elaborate use of gimp demonstrates some of the highest levels of skill seen in the Ipswich lace making. Black silk, ca. 1789–1790. *Courtesy of the Library of Congress, Washington, D.C.*

*Fig. 60.* This piece of Ipswich lace has two gimp threads and mock tally filling. Black silk, ca. 1789–1790. *Courtesy of the Library of Congress, Washington, D.C.*

Most of the pieces show a gimp that is attached with two twists coming from the ground and one twist going into the fill. Fig. 60 shows the use of a double gimp that does not have a twist between the two gimp threads. Other examples have a twist between the gimp threads, as in figs. 56 and 57.

Take a look at the clover pattern in fig. 58. It demonstrates one of the interesting facets of Ipswich lace: some pieces use the gimp in a cloth stitch to fill in and shape motifs, as often seen in the Blonde laces.

### The Header

The header is the decorative edge of the lace. The edges of Ipswich lace are straight or only slightly scalloped, typical of the Neoclassical laces of this period. (See figs. 43, 47, 50, 53, and 56.) The header edges show a great deal of variety, from well-thought-out and executed (see figs. 50 and 59) to rather thin and unusual examples (see figs. 47 and 58). Compared to the way Bucks was made in the mid-nineteenth century, the Ipswich header seems very thin. There are many reasons for this, including the fact that pairs are usually not usually carried along the header and in and out of the valleys as is the custom with modern Bucks. Instead, the stitches used in the valleys show many interesting solutions, variations, and creative techniques. Some valleys contain small touches such as a single "spider," a single Torchon ground stitch with an extra twist at the pin, or several pairs joined in whole stitches.

*The Picots*

A picot is small decorative loop found on the header edge of the lace. The picots in Ipswich lace are made with three to seven twists, depending on the piece of lace. The average number of twists is five. Many of the laces have loops that are imitations of picots (see fig. 47) that appear to have been done by less experienced workers.

Case Study 1

Fig. 61 shows a very good example of Ipswich lace from the collection at the Library of Congress. It is made of black silk thread of the type used

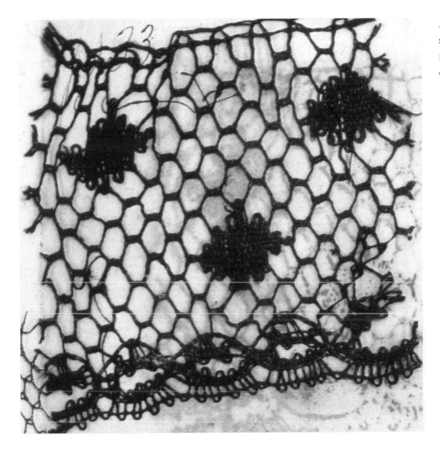

*Fig. 61.* Black silk Ipswich lace, ca. 1789– 1790. *Courtesy of the Library of Congress, Washington, D.C.*

in the other samples of Ipswich lace from the same period. This piece was worked with the footside on the left. The ground shows the typical distortions of an irregular grid. The ground stitch is of the Brussels type. The diamond-shaped designs in the groundwork are cloth stitch employing gimp threads that are not continuous. The unusual edge design is seen repeatedly in Ipswich laces. It is done with a cloth stitch that is worked around openings. The gimp is attached by twists on both sides, two on the ground side and one on the fill side. The header shows a nearly straight edge. And the picots are not real picots at all; they are loops clearly used to give the illusion of a picot. All of these features are typical of Ipswich lace.

Case Study 2

Oral tradition alleges that the pattern seen in figs. 62 and 63 was an original design created in Ipswich. Regardless, this piece makes an interesting study. Again, the piece was worked with the footside on the left. The Torchon-type ground shows the distortions of an uneven grid. Knots are clearly visible, and little effort was made to conceal the cut ends of the gimp threads. The dominant fill is the half stitch. The most unusual feature of this piece is the use of a type of spider pattern fill (see fig. 63). The piece shows a great deal of inconsistency and tension problems typical of a less skilled maker. Notice the uneven half stitch in the filling. The attachment of the gimp is very inconsistent. It has twists on either side, but the number of twists appears to have little rhyme or reason. The use of gimp is noncontinuous throughout the piece, and a double gimp is attached without a twist between the parallel gimp threads. The header has a very shallow scallop. The straight or nearly straight edge is typical of the period in which this piece was made. Notice how thin and sparse the header edge looks without the carried pairs running along the edge. This piece does employ picots. The design appears to be a watered-down style more typical of the third quarter of the eighteenth century.

This piece, which is in the Library of Congress, matches a pricking in the collection of the Whipple House in Ipswich, Massachusetts. Compare this piece to fig. 50, worked by a more experienced hand; the latter is much more even, and the gimp and design elements are more detailed.

This study of Ipswich lace shows the range of possibilities in late-eighteenth-century commercial lace. Pat Earnshaw's *A Dictionary of Lace* states that the English Bucks Point lace in "early forms may have had a wire, Torchon, or Mechlin reseau [groundwork]" (p. 25). This is a fair

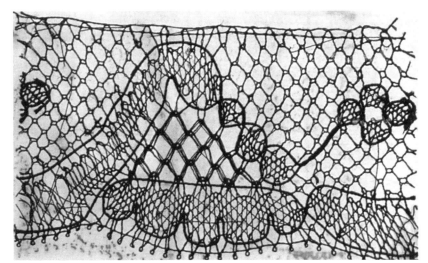

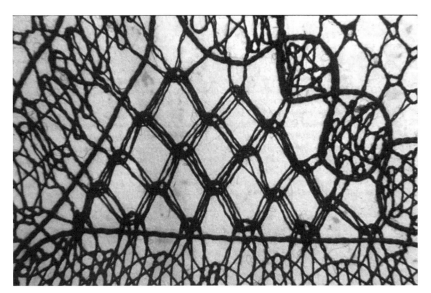

description of the grounds used in the Ipswich lace. It would make sense that Ipswich lace makers immigrating from this region, which they did, would be putting these grounds in their lace. While the techniques may be English, the style is not Bucks. Several excellent modern-day lace makers see designs and techniques in Ipswich lace making that are more reminicent of Continental laces; others see European influences that had an impact on lace making in general. Certainly, Ipswich lace bears witness to many influences.

While there is some evidence of the existence of Bucks Point as early as the sixteenth century, this lace reached its maturity or became fully developed in the mid-nineteenth century. What is now defined as Bucks is measured by the standards and characteristics of nineteenth-century Bucks. Less is known about Bucks point made in the eighteenth century or earlier. In all likelihood, the techniques used in making Ipswich lace reflect an interesting period in the development of Bucks before the nineteenth century. This would explain many of the features of the lace that deviate from nineteenth-century Bucks.

Even Torchon, which began showing up in portraits as early as 1610, did not reach maturity until the nineteenth century. Since it would be futile to try to force a nineteenth-century standard on eighteenth-century lace, the more productive avenue is understanding the characteristics that make up Ipswich lace itself. Early laces have a charm of their own and make fascinating study. It is especially interesting to discover at what point particular stitches were developed and to see how early lace makers solved or handled the technical problems faced by every lace maker. Such information is significant to lace history as well as enjoyable. A piece of lace that captures a period in the development of a particular type of lace is a bit of history, documented in thread instead of ink. Ipswich is that kind of lace.

3. IPSWICH LACE

1. Elizabeth M. Kurella, *The Secrets of Real Lace* (Kalamazoo, Mich.: The Printmill, 1994), p. 11.

2. Frances Morris, *Notes on Laces of the American Colonists* (New York: William Helburn for The Needle and Bobbin Club, 1926), p. 8.

3. Santina M. Levey, *Lace: A History* (London: Victoria and Albert Museum, 1983), p. 77. The author devotes an entire chapter to the Neoclassical period, a scholarly and informative presentation.

4. Pat Earnshaw, *A Dictionary of Lace* (Shire Publications, 1982), p. 66.

5. Judyth L. Gwynne, *The Illustrated Dictionary of Lace* (Berkeley, Calif.: Lacis Publications, 1997), p. 206.

6. Pamela Nottingham, *The Technique of Bucks Point Lace* (New York: Larousse and Co., 1981), p. 12.

7. Doris Southard, *Lessons in Bobbin Lace Making* (New York: Dover Publications, 1977), p. 57.

8. The term "Spanish ground" led to research on Spanish laces. The same ground that is found in Ipswich lace is indeed found in Spanish laces of the period. See Florence Lewis May, *Catalogue of Laces and Embroideries in the Collection of*

*the Hispanic Society of America* (New York: Hispanic Society of America, 1936), pp. H5958, H5959, H5956.

    9.  Gwynne, *Illustrated Dictionary of Lace*, pp. 42–44, 114–17, 198.

    10.  Pamela Nottingham, *The Technique of Bucks Point Lace* (New York: Larousse and Co., 1981), pp. 66–69.

# THE LACE MAKERS OF IPSWICH

*So ready and brisk with her hands . . . she earned, by making lace, a silk dress for each of her daughters.*                    —Caldwell Family Records

*T*HERE IS A STORY hidden within every piece of lace. The fine details woven into a piece of lace such as a knot used to repair a broken thread, the faltering variations of a novice, and the evident skills of a practiced hand tug at natural curiosity. If only artifacts could reveal the details of their making and more of the lives of their makers. What these artifacts can tell us are stories of the women and girls who made Ipswich lace. No record of Ipswich lace would be complete without acknowledging the women who made it.

*Elizabeth Lord Lakeman*

The lace pillow of Elizabeth Lord Lakeman in fig. 64 exemplifies a classic Ipswich pillow with lace in the process of being made. On an early spring day in her ninety-fourth year, Elizabeth worked on this piece of lace, crossing and twisting threads, placing pins, and adjusting tension. It was to be the last day of a long and adventurous life.

A card that is now with the pillow reads, "She lived to be over 90, worked on this pillow the day she died. She feared she lacked 'dying grace' but God took her while she knelt in prayer." This long life included working in the Ipswich lace industry to help her family.

The lace on the pillow is one of the most commonly made types of lace made in Ipswich. It is not surprising that at the age of 94 she was working on white lace, as white threads are much easier on the eyes than black threads. That she made both white and black lace is confirmed by the pricking for black lace that is part of her kit.

Her pillow has a newer covering that she added in later years, but the rest of the pillow is constructed of the same materials used in other Ipswich pillows. The pillow is fully dressed with pricking, pins, and lace in process. Although most of the bobbins have fallen off because threads break over time, one bobbin remains. It is attached to the gimp thread and

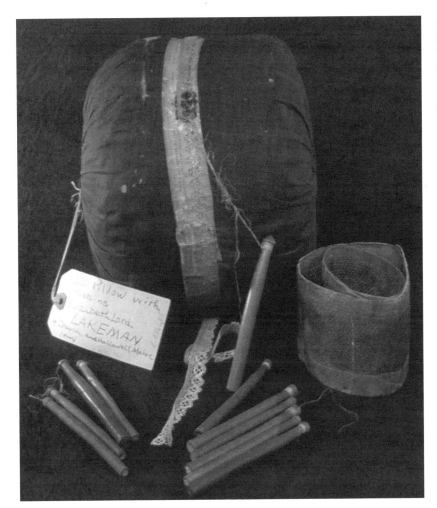

*Fig. 64.* The lace pillow and lace tools of Elizabeth Lord Lakeman, ca. 1789–1862. *Courtesy of the National Museum of American History.*

has not broken off because gimp thread is much thicker than the threads used to construct the rest of the lace. Elizabeth's bobbins—there are eleven remaining with her kit—are identical in all ways to the other Ipswich bobbins of this period.

Elizabeth's life began in 1767 in Ipswich where she was baptized on October 18,[1] the same year the embargoes began and tension between England and the colonies was peaking. At the tender age of nine years her world changed. She witnessed the American Declaration of Independence, and she knew the absence of her father in the Revolutionary War. By the time she was sixteen years old, the Treaty of Paris had been signed, and she saw America take its first steps as a new and independent nation. This woman grew up with America. She lived the earliest years of our history. At thirty-two she mourned with her country the death of the beloved George Washington and a year later, saw with fear and excitement the dawning of a new century. As time passed, she would know grief and mourn the loss of her infant son. At ninety-four years, she had been a wife, a mother, a neighbor, a friend, and one of the lace makers of Ipswich.

Elizabeth lived her early years with her parents, James and Elizabeth Lord. Her middle-class world was one of reasonable comfort as her father, known as "the Older Soldier," was a respected veteran of the American Revolution and the French and Indian Wars. He had a commission as lieutenant that was signed by John Hancock.[2] Her meals were very different from the expectations of the twenty-first century. The biggest meal of the day was served when the town bell rang at noon or just "half-past"; the morning and evening meals were more often broth from boiled meats with meal added or a porridge made from peas or beans. Even her writing would have been difficult for people in later centuries to read. Her *s* would have looked like an *f*, her spelling would have varied (spelling was not yet standardized), and the usage of words would be strange to our ear. This assumes that she had some sort of education in the skills of reading and writing, which was not always the case, especially for women and girls.

As a girl in her parents' keeping, she would have learned lace making —from her mother, an aunt, or a neighbor. Education for women of the eighteenth century was limited. Girls were often sent to another home to provide domestic service for an agreed period, helping with daily tasks and caring for children. In return she would gain valuable training in the domestic skills from the women of the household. This service benefited the overworked women of the household and also served to educate the girl and reinforce the bonds of neighbors and the community. Much of the fabric of early American life was structured around these communal bonds and the value of being a good neighbor.[3] In working as a helper many girls learned to weave, sew, darn, knit, and spin. In Ipswich the girls would have had the opportunity to learn lace making in addition to these other skills. Each girl's level of skill would vary greatly, depending on the skill of the woman who taught her. There was no lace school in Ipswich. Some girls had the good fortune to learn from an accomplished lace maker, and others learned from those newer to the trade.

Elizabeth's work shows that she was a skilled lace maker, even at an advanced age. It is interesting to note that the lace on her pillow is worked with the footside on the left, which is consistent with other Ipswich laces. By the time Elizabeth was making the last piece on her pillow, English laces of this type were being made with the footside on the right. It makes sense, though, that she continued to keep the footside on the left and to make lace in the manner in which she first learned the skill.

In 1788, when Elizabeth was twenty-one, her parents and younger siblings moved to Litchfield, Maine.[4] She stayed behind in Ipswich and worked with the other women involved in the lace-making industry. Elizabeth's level of skill allowed her to make the black as well as the white laces.

Her pricking for the black laces, as seen in fig. 65, was made of pasteboard identical to the other pasteboard prickings from Ipswich, which is a precise match to the sample of lace, in fig. 66, in part of the collection

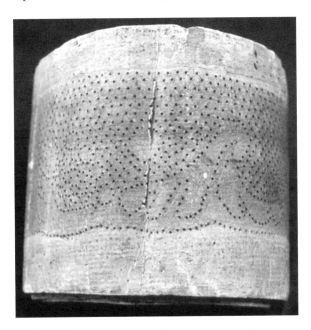

*Fig. 65.* Large pasteboard pricking, linen, ca. 1800 or earlier, from the lace kit of Elizabeth Lord Lakeman. Pricking matches lace in fig. 66. *Courtesy of the National Museum of American History.*

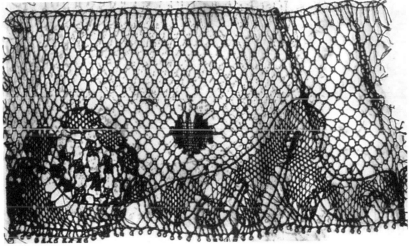

*Fig. 66.* Ipswich lace that matches the pricking used by Elizabeth Lord Lakeman, as shown in fig. 65. Black silk, ca. 1789–1790. *Courtesy of the Library of Congress, Washington, D.C.*

included with Joseph Dana's letter. It is possible that this sample of lace came from Elizabeth's pillow. However, no record has been found that can confirm whether it was from her pillow or from another that happened to have the same pattern. What is certain is that she was making this pattern in Ipswich during the time when Joseph Dana was collecting data and lace samples in response to George Cabot's inquiry. Elizabeth would have been about twenty-two, which is consistent with the level of skill demonstrated in this sample of lace. It is interesting to note that the technical details of the lace Elizabeth made at the age of ninety-four matches those of the sample of black lace mentioned above.

Elizabeth's reason for staying in Ipswich when her family left probably had a lot to do with a young man, Thomas Lakeman. Later in 1789 the notice of their intention to marry was published,[5] and the wedding took place on July 8, 1790. Elizabeth's life became busy with the duties of housekeeping and motherhood with her first two sons, Thomas, baptized June 9, 1791, and John, baptized October 21, 1792. When Elizabeth was twenty-six years old, she took her two boys and followed her husband, a brick mason, to Hallowell, Maine, where they lived on what is now Winthrop Street.[6] At the time she was seven months pregnant with her first daughter, Anna. She bore five more children, one of whom, Brown, died at the age of only nine months.[7]

Elizabeth was a typical eighteenth-century New England woman who lived her life as a wife and mother and who also happened to be a lace maker. If it were possible to know more about her, there undoubtably would be many interesting things to learn about her talents and life.

It is worth noting that, by the chance of fate in Hallowell, Maine, Elizabeth met Martha Ballard, another eighteenth-century New England woman, who, like Elizabeth, was also a wife and mother. Martha was a midwife whose diary has become well known and studied in great depth. Her journal is one of the best source documents of everyday life, as it is filled with the nuances of ordinary living, the work of a midwife, and the practice of medicine in the late eighteenth and early nineteenth centuries.

The connection between these two women is that Martha Ballard delivered Elizabeth Lord Lakeman's fifth son, Moses Bradstreet. She entered a brief note in her diary on December 7, 1798, of the birth of a fourth son, the fifth child to Mrs. Lakeman. Although this is the only reference to Elizabeth in Martha Ballard's diary,[8] it is interesting to note, two hundred years later, that the lives of these two ordinary women touched. Martha Ballard would likely be astounded at modern-day interest in her diary, just as Elizabeth would probably have blushed a bit at the thought of having her lace so closely studied. It is fortunate that some fragments and works of their hands have survived to allow for a greater understanding of their lives.

Women often made lace in their single years and before having children. The demands of motherhood were heavy, but as the children grew, many women went back to their lace pillows. At some point, Elizabeth did the same, although after the birth of Daniel she may have had some help. The Hallowell census of 1800 records there were four males under the age of 10 years in the household of Thomas Lakeman, as well as one male between 26 and 45 years, one female under 10 years, one female between 10 and 16 years, and one female between 26 and 45 years. The four males under the age of 10 were probably young Thomas, John, James, and Moses. The one male between 26 and 45 years would have been Thomas, Sr.; the one female under 10 years would have been Anna; and the one female between 26 and 45 years would have been Elizabeth, who was pregnant with Daniel. That accounts for everyone in the family except the one female between 10 and 16 years, which was most likely a neighbor or relative who had come as a helper to do domestic service.

Over the span of Elizabeth's life the world had changed dramatically. Lace making was more than something she happened to do. It was a constant in a life that had seen many ups and downs and its fair share of the wisdom that comes from living.

There were many lace-making families in Ipswich: the Caldwells, Lakemans, Lords, Suttons, Russells, Hodgkinses, Pitmans, Pulsiphers, Treadwells, Fosters, and Jewetts, to name only a few.


*Elizabeth Foster Sutton*

Mrs. Elizabeth Foster Sutton, the daughter of Nathaniel and Elizabeth Foster, was born December 1, 1736,[9] and became one of the most highly skilled of Ipswich's lace makers. A sweet passage in the Caldwell family records recalls with great fondness, "Elizabeth [Foster] was a notable housekeeper. So ready and brisk with her hands, as tradition has it, that she earned, by making lace, a silk dress for each of her daughters. And a still pleasanter tradition is, that her husband was so interested in observing her ready fingers on a quilt at a quilting bee, that he selected her at once as his companion for life."[10] Elizabeth appears to have been one of those industrious women whom others held in great fondness and respect.

At the time of Elizabeth's birth the first month of the year was March instead of January. This practice continued until January 1, 1752. Some years later, Elizabeth and Richard Sutton were married on October 19, 1758. Earning a silk dress for each daughter was no small feat, considering that they had a total of seven children, five of whom were girls. Richard Sutton, a leather dresser and maker of leather breeches[11] and a veteran of several wars,[12] lived his days with his family until his death on December 12, 1825, at the age of eighty-seven.

Elizabeth, with hands never idle, became the matriarch of one of Ipswich's largest lace-making families. One of her daughters, Mary, born November 24, 1771, grew up to become an Ipswich lace merchant. She would gather up the lace once a week from the lace makers, examine it for quality, and then take it to market by stagecoach. The lace was delivered as far north as Portsmouth and as far south as Boston. From Boston it was sold and exported to other areas, such as New York.

*The Trading of Goods and Services*

Mary Sutton was involved in more than the network of making and selling lace. She was part of an economic system that had been developing since the first English foot was placed on American soil. In Mary's lifetime the system was more sophisticated than simple bartering in that account books recorded transactions of purchases and payment of debts. Everyone lived on a system of credit and the exchange of goods and services. This meant that merchants would keep a tab or an account of the goods purchased; the settlement of these debts, or reckoning, would happen as season and fortune allowed.

Accounts were rarely paid in cash; more often they were paid in services or with goods of equivalent value. This tradition in Ipswich goes back to 1640, and town records declare: "As trade and commerce are embarrassed for want of money, no persons are to be compelled to pay future debts in cash, but in corn, cattle, fish, and other articles."[13] Thus, the tradition of paying in kind became the routine method of doing business. Many debts in Ipswich were paid in lace. Lace was traded for butter, flour, sugar, eggs, molasses, rum, chocolate, pork, potatoes, meal, salt, and specialty items such as silk, French calicoes, and even, on occasion, snuff.

The records of the Dames School,[14] run by Mrs. Lucy Kinsman Jewett between 1802 and 1811 and later by Miss Abigail, daughter of Joseph Dana, in the northwest upper room of his house, demonstrated this exchange of goods and a curious mix of coinage from the Old English shillings and pence to American dollars and even Spanish milled dollars. The change from the English monetary system to American dollars began in 1785. For many years after this date the old tender continued to be used. Mrs. Jewett charged nine pence a week for older children and eight pence a week for care of babies. Her accounting records showed that these debts were paid with milk, butter, cheese, eggs, apples, coffee, candles, bayberry tallow, beef at eight cents a pound, other meats, and fish; and "a long hard day's work by a woman was reckoned at forty-two cents." Frequent entries show tuition being paid by pillow lace valued at fifty cents a yard.

*Male versus Female Economic Systems*

Within the system of credit and payment in kind there existed another system, which distinguished between the economic endeavors of men and women. Most commerce was male-dominated, like the rest of society, politics, and religion; this is fairly well documented. But the work of women and exchanges of goods between women rarely found their way into written records. This factor alone makes the industry of lace making at Ipswich a fascinating study in the work of women.

A sample of transactions from the account books of men reveals trade in products such as wood, meat, meal, grains, or livestock for the farmer and mugs, shot, fabrics, paper, and "sundries" for the dry goods merchants. The trading of eggs, butter, and cheese or the services of wet nursing and domestic help occurred more often between women, a practical system that provided for more than the acquisition of staple goods. This system of depending on one another for assistance or goods provided a bond between families and neighbors, a bond so strong in the eighteenth century that no one ever had to worry about being left alone to suffer through an illness. Neighbors coming to help in times of need was a certainty.

Much of Ipswich lace was "sold" in this daily ebb and flow of the exchange of goods and services between women and their neighbors. When someone came to call, she often brought a gift such as fresh vegetables from the garden, a nicely baked pudding, or eggs. The phrase "much obliged," which today vaguely sounds like a quaint way to say thank you, came from this time and literally meant "I'm obligated." Such gifts were reciprocated with one of equal value. These exchanges were a routine and ordinary part of everyday living. Town life revolved around such interactions. The trading of Ipswich lace grew out of this very fundamental factor of eighteenth-century New England life.

### The Market for Lace

Letters and written documents indicate that lace was sold right off the lace maker's pillow, gathered up, and taken to market by stage. Or dealers sought out the lace makers of Ipswich directly. In an unpublished letter, Sarah E. Lakeman, a descendant of Elizabeth Foster Sutton, reports that Mrs. Thomas Caldwell of Ipswich received samples of popular lace from dealers. This dealer would have been a dry goods merchant like John Lakeman in Boston or Thomas Otis, who dealt mostly in lace. The samples of lace would be used to make prickings, and the lace makers would then make their own versions of the lace. Miss Lakeman reports that some women did nothing but make prickings and were paid up to ten cents for the more elaborate ones.

Despite the oral tradition that some merchants sought out the lace of the makers, recorded purchases of threads and pins indicate that individual lace makers were responsible for buying their own supplies. At least in the earlier period of the industry there is no evidence that the lace makers were directly employed by dealers or merchants. The early system was one run by women in which "lace merchants," women in their group like Mary Sutton, would gather up the lace once a week and take it to market.

### New Organization

By the time of Joseph Dana's writing a curious shift had taken place. All lace transactions disappeared from any remaining account books in Ipswich. And the tools for lace making became very standardized, as can be seen in a large proportion of surviving pillows and bobbins. What this indicates is that the individual no longer obtained her own tools; the tools were made in one central location and then distributed to the lace makers.

Some of the lace-making tools from the early period demonstrate a moderate amount of variety in style and materials. Later the majority of the tools (dated by the life dates of their owners) became remarkably similar. The shift seems to have occurred around the time of Joseph Dana's accounting and into the early nineteenth century. The development of the machine industry began with The Boston and Ipswich Lace Co., incorporated on February 4, 1826.[15]

Commission merchants most likely got involved when they realized the potential for profit in the growing market for lace. Profit may well have been the driving force behind the development of the machine-lace industry as well. The Heard family, especially George W. and Augustine, were well aware of the lace industry; they set up the first machine-lace company and were neighbors of Joseph Dana. The two factors were probably more than a coincidence.

Economic motivations remained a consistent theme in the lace industry. Many of the laces were known by their market value, such as "two and three penny lace." Lace had one significant advantage over other products in that large amounts of it could be rolled up into very small and valuable bundles that were quite handy to take to market. Even a frail or elderly woman could transport a sizable amount of lace to market, and many women in Ipswich used this to their advantage.

## Widow Pitman

Mrs. Mary Pitman, a widow, in 1767 paid her debt in part to Ezekiel Dodge, an Ipswich dry goods merchant, "by 6 [yards of] lace." (Notice, in figs. 67 and 68, that in eighteenth-century account books the word *to*, customarily on the left, refers to what is being purchased, and the word *by*, customarily on the right, refers to how the debt was paid. From the account of Mrs. Pitman, it appears that she supported herself by spinning and making lace, in exchange for which she purchased flour, molasses, sugar, flour, pork, rum, and sundries. She also appears to have liked chocolate.

## Mrs. Harris

Lace making, like other marketable skills, went a long way toward helping women support themselves and their families, especially in times of need. A bit of the oral tradition of Ipswich was conveyed by Frances Morris:

> How much these small earnings meant in the simple life of the sturdy
> New England women during the terrible years of the War of the Revolution is told in the story of one of the Ipswich lace makers, a Mrs. Harris,
> who, by her industry, supported a family of five children for over three
> years during the imprisonment of her husband who refused to swear

*Fig. 67.* Account of Widow Mary Pitman from the account book of Ezekiel Dodge, a dry goods merchant in Ipswich, ca. 1767–1768. This is the lefthand page of the account book, which records "to," or the items purchased. *Pitman Account — Photograph courtesy Peabody Essex Museum.*

allegiance to the King. Harris was confined in Dartmoor prison and every six months when taken out to test his loyalty, would only reply, "Damn your King and Parliament too!"[16]

This story about Mrs. Harris is typical of writings from the Colonial Revival. While it is true that New England women could be considered "sturdy," the phrase "simple life" does not apply and is something Mrs. Harris would have vigorously rejected. The lives of women in the eighteenth century were never simple.

The information in this story originated with the oral tradition as passed down by Sarah E. Lakeman. The story clearly has been embellished along the way. Miss Lakeman states in her writings that Mrs. David Harris traded lace for staples, such as potatoes, pork, and meal, from farming towns outside of Ipswich while her husband was detained at Dartmoor for three years and nine months. Although the story does have several points of truth and interest, there are some problems with the version as it has been passed down. David Harris was only three years old in 1776, and Dartmoor prison wasn't built until 1806, some twenty-three years after the formal end of the American Revolution.

A more accurate account would note that after coming to the aid of the Americans, the French had a revolution of their own. This gave rise to Napoleon, who fought tirelessly with the British. The British response was to open Dartmoor prison in 1809 to house French prisoners.

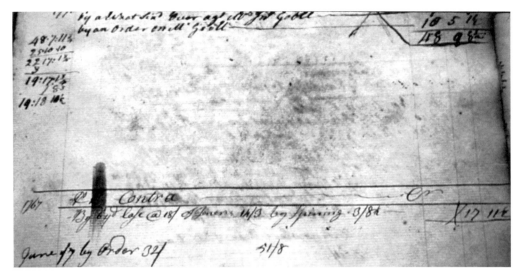

*Fig. 68.* Righthand page of the account book carrying the account of Widow Mary Pitman. This page records "by," or how the debts were settled. *Pitman Account—Photograph courtesy Peabody Essex Museum.*

Meanwhile, Britain was involved in heated disputes with the Americans about trade issues. Thus began the War of 1812, which gave Britain the opportunity to solve both their trade problems and their need for more sailors in their battle with France. The solution was to seize American ships and crews, which sent a clear message to Americans doing trade with France or in the Mediterranean. The captured men were given the somewhat dubious choice to either join or be pressed into service with the British ranks and fight the French or go to Britain's new prison at Dartmoor. Those that they could enlist in the battle with France helped solve their manpower problem, and they justified imprisoning the others by declaring that any American male who had lived during the American Revolution could, from their perspective, still be considered a British subject. When American ships were captured by the British, it was very difficult to tell the British from the Americans without documentation. They talked, dressed, and looked the same. Therefore, unless a man of about the age of forty could prove otherwise, he was considered British.

David Harris got caught in this trap because he found himself in the wrong place at the wrong time and fell victim to the costs of war. As a forty-year-old seaman doing trade in 1812 he took the same risks of capture and confrontation with Britain as did his fellow countrymen who engaged in this type of commerce. Fortunately, he survived his experience (census records document his residency in Massachusetts as late as 1855 at the age of 82 years). Harris was the right age for the British to justify his imprisonment by declaring him a British subject, which makes sense of the statement that "every six months when taken out to test his loyalty, [he] would only reply, 'Damn your King and Parliament too!'" As an American, he naturally would refer to the English king as *your King*. He apparently was unable to document his American citizenship and stayed at Dartmoor for an extended period.

At the time of this writing, new records have been discovered that support this account. At the National Archives in Washington, D.C., there are records of imprisoned men in the War of 1812. Included in those records is the listing of prisoners from Dartmoor prison. In the roster, Depot Entry number 2311, is the name of David Harris. He was on a private vessel named the *Saturn* under sail at "Sandy Hook," when his ship was captured and his crew taken on May 25, 1814.[17]

Surviving reports state that Mr. Harris died on May 5, 1863,[18] having lived into his nintieth year. Mrs. David Harris, born Sarah Emmons, did stay home through those years and lace making is most likely a true part of her story. She would have done what most women in her circumstances would do: care for her family using all the skills she knew, including lace making.

*Homespun Valor*

The David Harris account attests to the fact that eighteenth-century life was filled with stark realities. Enormous efforts were required to make the rocky New England land productive while at the same time being involved in seemingly endless battles. Waves of conflict such as the French and Indian Wars, disputes over taxation, the American Revolution, and the War of 1812—not to mention conflicts between France and England, both which demanded that Americans not engage in trade with the other—took their toll.

It is interesting to note that the most productive years of the lace industry coincide with these conflicts, not so much because war had any direct impact on the industry but because Ipswich used lace making as a way to endure through such times. Ipswich women simply took advantage of a domestic market developed out of trade disputes. They sustained themselves through long separations from their husbands and the other men in their families. The way they maintained their families and homes under such conditions speaks volumes about their spirit and determination. Our century looks upon these women with admiration.

From their perspective they did the most ordinary of things. They survived.

## Spirit

There seems to be a little more than economics to the lace industry. It is important not to project twenty-first-century thoughts of independence on the minds of eighteenth-century women, but there appear to be both social and mildly political factors involved in lace production. The world of politics was undoubtably the exclusive domain of men. Abigail Adams, who was herself a lace maker, was a woman who had given politics some serious consideration, but most women ignored politics and went on with their daily lives, perhaps experiencing a sense of patriotism rather than involvement in politics. The issue of women's patriotism expresses itself eloquently in the *Salem Gazette* of January 31, 1782, in an open letter published by a frustrated Englishman who laments to a friend in London his discovery that the local women of Charlestown prefer their "homespun manufactures" and "despise the gay toys which are imported here." He goes on to say, "An officer told Lord Cornwallis not long ago that if he had destroyed all the men in North America, we should have enough to do to conquer the women." It seems that the making and wearing of homespun manufactures or domestically produced goods such as Ipswich lace connoted more than the driving force of economics. It will be up to social historians to determine if such things were a political statement, a simple testament of pride, or a unified rejection of England's domination.

## Social Changes

Whether women did or did not involve themselves in politics, one point is clear: the world of women changed significantly during the American Revolution. More than a revolution of political ideology, it was a social revolution as well, and the social changes made the development of the lace industry possible. Attitudes about personal rights and the roles of women began to change. Women were not as tightly bound to their homes; they had more opportunity to trade goods at market. For the women of Ipswich that meant traveling beyond their homes and towns to trade lace in the surrounding mercantile towns.

When the industry existed has been a topic of some speculation mixed with contradictory published information. It is not surprising that there has been much confusion over this issue. A history of Ipswich states: "As early as 1692, a writer observed, of this Ipswich industry, 'Silk and thread lace of an elegant and lasting texture are manufactured in large quantities by women and children and sold for use and exportation.'"[19] This quote has mistakenly given the impression that the lace-making industry of Ipswich began in the seventeenth century. It can now be demonstrated that lace making in Ipswich was an industry of the eighteenth and early nineteenth centuries. The knowledge that a lace-making industry did not and could not have existed in Ipswich in the seventeenth century puts into question the date of 1692 published in Waters's work. Frank Waters was known as a solid historian. In all cases his work has been meticulous and accurate, with the exception of this date. Was the 1692 date an error in publishing? Or does the date refer to lace making in general and not the industry?

Unfortunately, writings of this period in our history commonly lack the references and documentation of sources that is the current custom. Trying to find where Mr. Waters gained his information led to lengthy tracing of his writing to documents such as town records, deeds, wills, letters, published books, and archival records available to him. One of the writings he had access to was book by Joseph B. Felt, *The History of Ipswich, Essex, and Hamilton*, first published in 1834. Under the heading "manufacters," Mr. Felt wrote a passage very similar to the one found in Waters's work,

> *Lace.* This, of thread and silk, was made in large quantities and for a long period, by girls and women. It was formed on a lap-pillow, which had a piece of parchment round it with the particular figure, represented by pins stuck up straight, around which the work was done and the lace wrought. Black as well as white lace was thus manufactured of various widths, qualities, and prices.

> 1790. No less than 41,979 yard were made here annually. (p. 101)

Although this account does have the same information and uses some of the same phrases, it does not cite a date of 1692.

A further search found an even earlier work. As part of a journal of his travels, Jedidiah Morse wrote in the *American Gazetteer*: "Silk and thread lace, of an elegant texture, are manufactured here [Ipswich] by women and children, in large quantities, and sold for use and exportation in Boston, and other mercantile towns. In 1790 no less than 41,979 yards were made here, and the manufacture is rather increasing." Waters's account was nearly a direct quote from this work, and Morse clearly obtained his information from the report of Joseph Dana, including the amount of yardage sold in one year. The now well-known figure of 41,979 yards was obtained between 1789 and 1790, not 1692. Morse's account was published in 1797, when he visited Ipswich at the height of the industry.

A smaller text, *Fine Thread, Lace and Hosiery in Ipswich*, by Jesse Fewkes, and *Ipswich Mills and Factories*, by R. Frank Waters, shed a little light on where the 1692 date originated. This volume, which includes both titles and the *Proceedings of the Annual Meeting*, was published by the Ipswich Historical Society in 1903. On page 29, under mills and factories, Mr. Waters also mentions 1692 but this time with a reference to "Mr. M. V. B. Perley in his History of Ipswich, in History of Essex Country, Mass., Boston, 1878." Mr. Perley's book has not been found despite an exhaustive search of Ipswich archives, libraries in the surrounding area, and the Library of Congress. But we can assume that Mr. Waters was quoting Mr. Perley, who either was misinformed or was unclear about the dates of the industry. He may well have thought that any lace making qualified as part of the industry.

Even though we do not have Mr. Perley's book to review, the evidence clearly shows that Ipswich lace was not a seventeenth-century endeavor. This does not mean that there could not have been lace making in Ipswich before the industry.[20] Fragments of lace and town records show otherwise. Certainly, women immigrating to Ipswich brought their lace-making knowledge with them. However, a few women making lace for their own use and a lace-making industry involving more than six hundred women are two very different matters.


*Why Not the Seventeenth Century?*

The seventeenth century was a time when the world of women was severely restricted. In fact, all of life was restricted within the structured world of seventeenth-century Ipswich. Even people moving to Ipswich did not have liberty to take up residence without a vote of approval from the town. Men were not allowed to vote unless they owned property and were members of the church. The seriousness of these restrictions is clear in the town records of 1661: when "an inhabitant of Ipswich, living at a distance, absented himself with his wife from public worship, the General Court empowered the Seven men [a leadership group within the church] to sell his farm so that they may live nearer the sanctuary and be able more conveniently to attend on its religious services."[21]

During this time most settlers were focused on turning natural forest and rocky ground into fertile and productive land. Such an endeavor was no small task. Most of the men immigrating to New England came to gain wealth or financial independence, known as "competency." Owning productive land was the method employed to gain this status of independent wealth. Because so many people were following their own dreams for prosperity, few were available to be hired hands. Most men were busy working their own land, leaving few available for hire, and those who were willing to work for hire came at an unusually high rate. The resulting labor shortage forced men to turn to their families for help in the fields. Young men often stayed at home until they were in their thirties; in some cases the eldest son remained permanently to help work the land that would eventually become his own. This labor shortage alone did not offer women an opportunity to develop an industry. Their efforts were primarily employed in working the land and caring for their families.[22]

In addition, there are no artifacts or records from the seventeenth century that document an industry of lace making. A few artifacts verify only that some knew the skill of lace making and others were engaged in trade of imported lace. However, town records show that in 1634 an edict against making and wearing clothing embellished with lace became the law, a further hindrance to the development of a lace industry.

Besides helping work the land, women faced the challenges of clothing their families. Clothing was handmade from homespun threads and yarns that they grew themselves. Flax, hemp, and wool production was a staple of early Ipswich economy. To grow, process, spin, and weave fabric was a lengthy operation; then the clothing had to be made. A shortage of wool was an additional stumbling block. The 1645 edict ordering an increase in the sheep population was a response to this shortage.[23]

By 1651 another edict allowed the wealthy to wear lace and other finery but only if their estates were valued at two hundred pounds or more, a considerable sum in those times. Lace making became a legal employment, but the ready market would have been meager.

Problems of shortages were not quickly solved. In 1656 it was ordered that "the Selectmen are to divide their towns into classes of five, six, and ten, and appoint a class-leader, for the purpose of spinning. They are to assess each family a quarter, half, or whole spinner, according to its other occupation. Each family, which can furnish one spinner, shall spin for thirty weeks in a year."[24] Those that did not comply where fined twelve pence per month for each pound short. Flax and hemp seeds had to be saved, and the common was ordered cleared for sheep.[25] The wool shortage was so severe that sheep were not allowed to leave the town. It is clear that the burden of spinning was heavy, and failure was met with a high penalty. The women of Ipswich were busy spinning, supporting their land and crops, and caring for their families. No time would have been left for lace making.

Social expectations of the proper role for a woman or "goodwife" did not include traveling beyond her home and town to engage in the trading of lace. In any case, methods of transportation were few and far between. Most people walked. Horses were scarce in Ipswich until the middle of the eighteenth century. Owned and operated by John Stavers, the first coach, that stopped in Ipswich on its way to Boston, did not begin service until 1762.[26] Without a means of transportation the product could not reach its market.

A conclusive factor is the dating of laces. Ipswich laces were of the type made in the second half of the eighteenth century and the early nineteenth century, not the type made in the seventeenth century. The Whipple House has an interesting collection of laces that are worth study and conservation but have no connection with the industry. There are several pieces of classical laces such as Flemish, Mechlin, Maltese, and Bedfordshire in the collection that were donated to the Whipple House by Michael Auclair in the 1970s. One is a rather small but beautiful piece of Flemish lace circa 1640. This piece has nothing to do with the industry of Ipswich lace and was added to the collection purely out of the curator's interest in lace in general. The oldest laces have no connection with pillows, prickings, or bobbins of the type that would have been used to create Ipswich lace. This indicates that these older laces were imported and not made in Ipswich.

Perhaps it is an obvious point, but evidence for an industry includes a volume of remaining tools of the trade of a type consistent with commercial production. The tools and the skills of the people who made the lace should demonstrate that they had been used together to produce a certain style of lace.

In Ipswich the eighteenth-century artifacts and evidence of an industry fit these requirements. The volume of tools is adequate to show the existence of an industry. The types of tools are consistent with an industry because they are simple, unadorned, functional. The lace itself is of the type made at that time, it matches the existing tools, and it demonstrates a skill consistent with what would be expected from the eighteenth century or later. The prickings for Ipswich lace match the lace pinhole for pinhole. In short the lace fits the prickings, and in turn the prickings fit the pillows. Therefore, evidence shows that commercial production did not exist in the seventeenth century and just as strongly shows that it did exist in the eighteenth century.

*An Eighteenth-Century Industry*

An eighteenth-century industry makes more sense in view of the information now available. An abundance of artifacts and documents support the existence of an industry in the eighteenth and nineteenth centuries.

After the edicts of the seventeenth century were rescinded and the labor and clothing shortages were resolved, women had more time to apply themselves to other duties. The hard work of the seventeenth century had left productive fields. Women continued to assist with working the land, but the effort was not as difficult as it once had been. The restrictions of the seventeenth century softened as churches split and new ones were formed. Changes in the social order gave way to more concern about individuals' rights and somewhat less concern for authority. The embargoes of the 1760s and 1770s created a market for lace and discouraged the purchase of imported laces. Trade routes had been established between Ipswich and other mercantile towns. Stagecoaches routinely carried passengers to surrounding areas, allowing travel to other mercantile towns. The shortage of currency continued the dependence on the trading of goods and services instead of the use of cash, and lace was handy for such purposes. The tradition of cottage industries and domestic production was the normal standard. To date, all evidence of an industry affirms a direct link to the eighteenth and early nineteenth centuries, not the seventeenth century.

*A Lace Family*

One family of lace makers began with Elizabeth Foster Sutton, who was born in 1736. Her descendants exemplify a line of women involved in the lace industry. Elizabeth's five daughters were probably all involved in the

*Fig. 69.* Susan Lord (Russell) Lakeman in photograph taken December 25, 1903, when she was eighty-eight years old. The back of the photograph is signed "Susan L. Lakeman" in her own hand. *Courtesy, Ipswich Historical Society, Ipswich, Massachusetts.*

industry and learned the skills of lace making from their mother. Mary (1771–1825) certainly was involved in the industry as a lace merchant. Her sister Sarah (1775–1841), sometimes referred to as Sally, married Daniel Russell on February 28, 1793. They had four children, one of whom, Susan Lord Russell, had something unusual: she had a middle name. The use of middle names did not become popular until around 1783.

## Susan Lord (Russell) Lakeman

Susan Lord Russell, baptized on November 18, 1815, was one of the last Ipswich lace makers and one of the last eyewitnesses to the Ipswich lace industry. At age thirty she married Ebenezer Lakeman, a thirty-nine-year-old mariner on May 29, 1845.[27] By the time of her marriage she had become the matriarch of the family, having lost her mother and aunts. Susan died on September 4, 1905.

## Sarah E. Lakeman

The daughter of Susan Lord Russell and Ebenezer Lakeman, Sarah E. Lakeman (January 24, 1850–April 25, 1937) was noted for her lectures on lace and for passing on the oral traditions of the lace industry as she had learned them from her mother. Samples of Susan's lace housed at the

Whipple House and notes from Miss Lakeman's letters show that both mother and daughter made lace. Sarah E. Lakeman continued to make lace but was never involved directly with the industry.

She became instead an important local historian who worked hard to keep the memory of Ipswich's lace-making history alive. She gave lectures and worked with the historical society to preserve the Ipswich lace collection. A copy of one of her lectures is a handwritten account of the oral tradition of lace making in Ipswich and is still preserved at the Whipple House with other lace-related manuscripts. Archived records of the Ipswich Historical Society record a meeting on December 6, 1909, that was "called to order by the President T.F. Waters (author of the History of Ipswich) at 7:45 O'clock PM." This document notes the following: "Voted: that Miss S. E. Lakeman be made chairman of a lace committee."

Lydia Lord Lakeman

Fig. 70 shows the lace pillow of Lydia Lord Lakeman, born May 3, 1781,[28] one of the Ipswich lace makers on the paternal side of Sarah E. Lakeman's family. Lydia likely learned her lace-making skills from her mother, Susanna Kimball, wife of Daniel Lord Jr. Kimball is another family name that appears commonly among the lace-making families of Ipswich.

Lydia married Ebenezer Lakeman on December 22, 1803. Their son, also named Ebenezer Lakeman, married Susan Lord Russell, and they

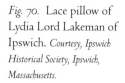

*Fig. 70.* Lace pillow of Lydia Lord Lakeman of Ipswich. *Courtesy, Ipswich Historical Society, Ipswich, Massachusetts.*

became the parents of Sarah E. Lakeman. Lydia Lord Lakeman was Sarah E. Lakeman's grandmother.

Lydia's pillow has seen a lot of history. First it was used in the industry, and then it was passed down to be kept as a treasure by Sarah E. Lakeman until she donated it to the Whipple House. Since that time it has been photographed and is published as plate 14 of Emily Noyes Vanderpoel's book *American Lace and Lace-Makers* and as plate B of Frances Morris's book, *Notes on Laces of the American Colonists*. In more recent times the pillow went through another transformation: in the mid-1970s, Michael Auclair added a new cover to the pillow and used one of the pasteboard prickings to re-create samples of the black Ipswich laces. The pillow will soon be on display at the Whipple House.

The laces and lace-making tools these women left behind have provided an abundance of information. Their skills and their tireless efforts to support their homes, families, and nation stand as a tribute to the spirit of American ingenuity. The lace makers of Ipswich were ordinary people who, by supporting their families, found themselves playing a part in forging a new nation and taking the first steps toward the industrialization of this country.

4. THE LACE MAKERS OF IPSWICH

1. Ipswich Vital Records, 1:242 (hereafter VR).

2. Abraham Hammatt, *The Hammatt Papers: Early Inhabitants of Ipswich, Massachusetts, 1633–1700* (Baltimore: Genealogy Publishing Co., 1980), p. 213.

3. For more information on this topic, see Laurel Thatcher Ulrich, *Good Wives: Image and Reality in the Lives of Women in Northern New England, 1650–1750* (New York: Alfred A. Knopf, 1982; reprint, New York: Vintage Books/Random House, 1991), and *A Midwife's Tale: The Life of Martha Ballard, Based on Her Diary, 1785–1812* (New York: Alfred A. Knopf, 1990; reprint, New York: Vintage Books, 1991).

4. Hammatt, *Hammatt Papers*, p. 213.

5. November 20, 1789, Ipswich VR:269

6. Charles Elventon Nash, *The History of Augusta; First Settlements and Early Days as a Town, Including the Diary of Mrs. Martha Moore Ballard, 1785 to 1812* (August, Me.: Charles E. Nash & Son, 1904), p. 377.

7. Anna, baptized August 12, 1794; James, baptized October 2, 1796; Moses Bradstreet, baptized December 7, 1798; Daniel Dodge, baptized December 20, 1800; Hannah Elizabeth, baptized April 9, 1807; and Brown, baptized March 8, 1809, Hallowell VR 6:96.

8. The story of the life of Martha Ballard is expertly researched and documented in Ulrich, *Midwifes's Tale.*

9. Ipswich VR: 1:144

10. Caldwell Family Records, collected and arranged by Augustine Caldwell, and published as *Caldwell Records* (Boston: William Parsons Lunt, 1873), p. 74

11. Thomas Franklin Waters, *Ipswich in Massachusetts Bay Colony, Vol. 1 1633–1700, Vol. 2 1700–1917* (Ipswich, Mass.: Ipswich Historical Society, 1917), pp. 259–60.

12. Ibid., p. 336; Caldwell Family Records, p. 74.

13. Joseph B. Felt, *History of Ipswich, Essex, and Hamilton* (Cambridge, Mass., 1834; reprint, Ipswich, Mass: Clamshell Press, 1966), p. 102.

14. Waters, *Ipswich,* pp. 531–34.

15. Ibid., pp. 632–33.

16. Frances Morris, *Notes on the Laces of the American Colonists* (New York: William Heilbrun, for The Needle and Bobbin Club, 1926), p. 13.

17. From the account of prisoners at Dartmoor prison by Robert G. Beasley, Esq., American Agent to American Prisoners in England, National Archives, Office of Naval Records, box 3566, RG. #45, stack area 11W4, row 16, compartment 3.

18. Ipswich VR:Holbrook Fiche #101.

19. Waters, *Ipswich,* p. 369.

20. For more information on lace making in America, see Emily Noyes Vanderpoel, *American Lace and Lake-Makers* (New Haven, Conn.: Yale University Press, 1924); and Morris, *Notes on Laces.*

21. Felt, *History of Ipswich,* pp. 57–58.

22. For more information on this topic, see Daniel Vickers, *Farmers and Fishermen: Two Centuries of Work in Essex County, Massachusetts, 1630–1850* (Chapel Hill: University of North Carolina Press, 1994).

23. Felt, *History of Ipswich,* p. 100.

24. Ibid.

25. Ibid.

26. Ibid., p. 31.

27. Ipswich VR:378.

28. Ipswich VR:245.

# A MATTER OF CLASS AND PRIDE

*A Tribute to Those Who Wore Ipswich Lace*

$\mathcal{M}$RS. DAVID HARRIS, Mary Sutton, Lydia Lord Lakeman, Elizabeth Lord Lakeman, Mary Boardman Caldwell, Mary Ann Jewett, Susan Kimball, Susan Lord Russell Lakeman, Lucy Lord, Elizabeth Foster Sutton, and others like them took the most common of daily activities, the production and exchange of goods, and by their ingenuity and a twist of fashion and fate created an industry unique in American history. These women were one part of the story of Ipswich lace. The women who wore the lace were the other. Portraits from the late eighteenth century illustrate not only *who* wore Ipswich lace but *how* they wore it.

### Sarah Noyes Chester

One lovely example of how Ipswich lace was worn is the portrait of Sarah Noyes Chester (1722–1797) of Wethersfield, Connecticut (see fig. 71). Her portrait was painted in 1796 and is attributed to Joseph Steward. In this portrait, Mrs. Chester is wearing two types of Ipswich black silk lace in her shawl. Even though Steward's representation of the lace is not meticulous, the clover leaf pattern (see fig. 71 a) is recognizable and bears a striking resemblance to a sample of Ipswich lace in the Library of Congress (see fig. 58). The other lace is a narrower pattern (see fig. 71 b) that can be matched to prickings located at the Whipple house in Ipswich, Massachusetts. Mrs. Chester may have gotten her lace while visting relatives in Ipswich (a branch of the Noyes family lived there). Or the lace could have found its way to Wethersfield by means of merchants who obtained their goods in Boston, where Ipswich lace was often taken for sale.

### Constant Storrs

The portrait of Mrs. Constant Storrs of Lebanon, New Hampshire, was painted in 1802 by William Jennys. (See fig. 72). Her lace-trimmed cap is

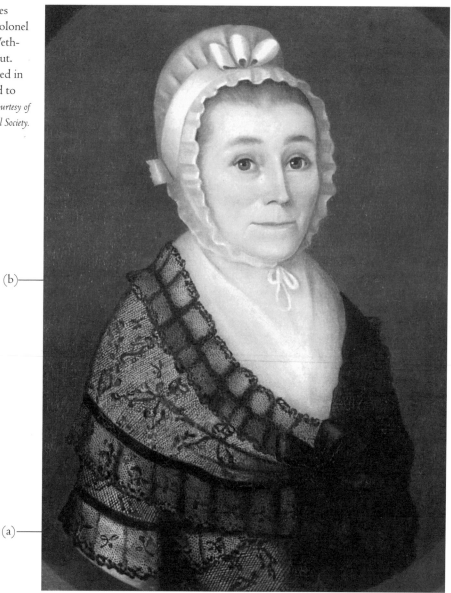

*Fig. 71.* Sarah Noyes Chester, wife of Colonel John Chester of Wethersfield, Connecticut. Oil on linen, painted in 1796 and attributed to Joseph Steward. *Courtesy of the Wethersfield Historical Society.*

(b)

(a)

of the style worn by mature women of this period and is a fine illustration of the use of the white laces. The lace on her cap is a good match to the lace on the cap in fig. 34. (Fig. 35 is a close up of the lace.) It is not surprising that Ipswich lace shows up in New England portraits. Mrs. Storrs was in the right location at the right time, and her social standing was consistent with those who wore Ipswich lace.

*Fig. 72.* Mrs. Constant
Storrs of Lebanon,
New Hampshire. Oil
on canvas, painted by
William Jennys probably
in 1802. *Courtesy of the Penn-
sylvania Academy of the Fine
Arts, Philadelphia. Gift of John
Frederick Lewis.*

*Mrs. Hezekiah Beardsley*

Another eighteenth-century portrait that illustrates Ipswich lace is that of
Mrs. Hezekiah Beardsley (born Elizabeth Davis, 1748/49–1790) (see fig.
73 a). The lace is again the black silk lace used on the edge of a shawl and
a very close match to the diamond pattern seen in a sample of Ipswich
lace at the Library of Congress. (See fig. 61.)

(a)

*An Issue of Class and Social Standing*

As more portraits and garments are being identified and studied, a pattern has developed that offers an important perception about the women
who wore the lace. Even paintings that do not show Ipswich lace hold significant information. The portrait of Mrs. Ezekiel Goldthwait in the
Museum of Fine Arts in Boston, painted by John Singleton Copley, exemplifies both the extraordinary skills of the artist and the dress of a
woman of the upper class. She wears the popular black lace shawl, but the
lace on her shawl is not Ipswich lace. Mrs. Goldthwait was from what

could be considered the aristocracy of Boston. The color (brown) of her dress symbolizes the highest rank of wealth and social standing, and the lace she wore was imported. Mmes Chester, Beardsley, and Storrs could be considered financially comfortable, but they were not from the high society of Mrs. Goldthwait. They were women of the middle to upper-middle class, and they did wear Ipswich lace.

The painters themselves demonstrate this distinction. While Jennys[1] and Steward, with varying degrees of success, sought to make a living with their artistic services, they were not in the same class as John Single-ton Copley, either in level of skill or in clientele. We can see that the wealthiest women continued to wear imported laces regardless of wars or embargoes. Meanwhile, women of the middle class wore Ipswich lace.

As handmade Ipswich lace satisfied the desire for finery in the growing American middle class, the coming of machine laces furthered this trend by making lace more affordable and readily available to the average American consumer. No longer was lace exclusively the symbol of great wealth.

Some find the unrefined details of the lace disappointing when compared to the lovely laces of Europe. What Ipswich lace makers accomplished under the most difficult of circumstances was a remarkable achievement: they created a new lace on American soil. European laces became refined through the work of many lace schools and through a noble and solid tradition, generation after generation. Ipswich lace never had that opportunity. By the time lace schools were being established in this country, the demand for handmade lace was in rapid decline, and machine laces were taking over the market. Gone were the days when lace was a status symbol and a sign of great wealth. Machines made it a product available to all.


*Martha Washington's Shawl*

Mrs. Washington's shawl is a typical "breakfast shawl" made from a collection of different black laces (see fig. 74). One of the laces is of particular interest. Fig. 75 is a close up look at a piece of lace that bears all the idiosyncrasies of other black Ipswich laces. This piece has exactly the same header shaping, ground, fills, designs, creative techniques, and gimp attachments as the other Ipswich laces. This particular design looks like a variation of one of the common designs used in the black Ipswich laces.

As we know, black silk lace was in fashion, and Martha was very fond of black lace as is evident in many of her portraits. George Washington

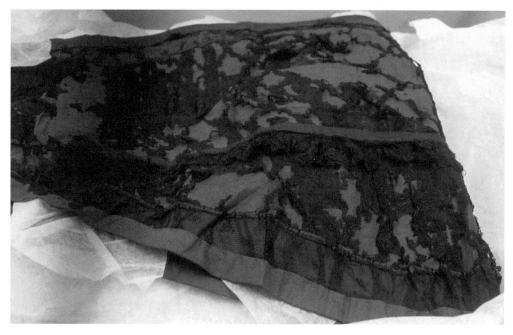

*Fig. 74.* Shawl owned by Martha Washington made with a combination of laces. *Courtesy of the Mt. Vernon Ladies' Association, gift of Miss Annie Burr Jennings.*

*Fig. 75.* Close-up of Ipswich lace on the shawl owned by Martha Washington. Black silk, ca. 1789. *Courtesy of the Mt. Vernon Ladies' Association, gift of Miss Annie Burr Jennings.*

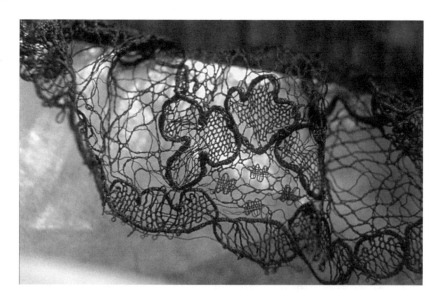

was very fond of lace as well, and he was an avid supporter of domestic textile manufacturing. On October 30, 1789, President George Washington made a trip to Newburyport, Massachusetts.[2] A surviving letter from George Cabot invites the president to make a stop and refresh himself in Beverly along his way.[3] George Cabot was involved in cotton manufacturing and by this time was well aware of the lace industry at Ipswich as he had secured the services of Joseph Dana to report to him on the annual production.

The president took Cabot up on his offer and was given a tour of the cotton mills. Later the same day, Mr. Washington made a stop in Ipswich on his way to Newburyport. Joseph Felt records the event in his book *History of Ipswich, Essex, and Hamilton*: "George Washington, on his visit to the North, is escorted into town; receives a short address; dines at the inn, then kept by Mrs. Homan; reviews a regiment, mustered to honor him; is visited by many; stays three hours, and leaves for Newbury, through lines of a multitude comprising both sexes of all ages, who had assembled to give him, with deep emotions of gratitude, a welcome and a parting look. Seldom is respect more heartily and deservedly rendered, than it was on this occasion."[4]

On this same occasion Rev. Augustine Caldwell presented a more personal view of Mr. Washington's response to the welcome at Ipswich: "He heard the Ipswich welcome; lifted his hat and graciously acknowledged it; and when at that moment a little Rebeckah was brought to him and introduced as the daughter of his late friend and officer, Col. Dodge, he laid his hand upon the head of the child and kissed her in memory of his friend, her father—an incident never forgotten by the crowd."[5] Mr. Washington made a lasting impression on the people of Ipswich.

We do not know whether the laces of Mrs. Washington's shawl were purchased or were from a collection given as gifts and conveniently at hand when such a garment was desired. What is known about the shawl is that it was purchased by Miss Annie Burr Jennings, vice-regent for Connecticut, in 1917 from Stan V. Henkels. She then presented the garment to the Mount Vernon Ladies Association. The documentation certificate with the shawl stated that it was worn by Mrs. Washington and inherited by Mrs. George R. Goldsborough, a descendant. It was then passed down to her half niece, Hortence Monroe McTabins, who sold it to the auctioneer, Mr. Henkels, and signed the authenticity note now in the records at Mount Vernon.

Judging by the types of laces on this shawl, it is likely that it was made some years after Mr. Washington's visit to Ipswich. It is interesting to note that the shawl's Ipswich lace has withstood the pressures of time much better than the other laces that comprise the garment. One last test was done in an effort to verify whether the lace was truly from Ipswich. Fiber analysis was done by the National Museum of American History. The lace in question was made of silk thread, as were all the other black Ipswich laces. A further analysis comparing fiber samples from Mrs. Washington's shawl with fibers from the documented samples of Ipswich laces at the Library of Congress showed that the silk thread was identical in both specimens. This piece of lace on Mrs. Washington's shawl, in the best judgment of science and reason, is Ipswich lace.

### Abigail Winship Robbins

The cape in fig. 76 was worn by Abigail Winship Robbins. She became a widow in 1795, when her husband, William Robbins, was lost on a fishing trip along with his friend Samuel Wait. Black capes were popular, along with other black garments, gloves, and gold rings, for funerals and mourn-

*Fig. 76.* Woman's cape, worn by Abigail Winship Robbins, late eighteenth or early nineteenth century, black silk with black silk lace. Lace is Ipswich of the type made in the late eighteenth century. *Courtesy, Museum of Fine Arts, Boston. Reproduced with permission. © 2000 Museum of Fine Arts, Boston. All rights reserved. Gift of Miss Ellen A. Stone.*

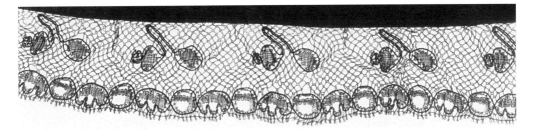

*Fig. 77.* Detail of lace on woman's cape, late eighteenth or early nineteenth century, Ipswich lace made of black silk. This piece matches the lace sample in fig. 52 and pricking that is in Ipswich. *Courtesy, Museum of Fine Arts, Boston. Reproduced with permission. © 2000 Museum of Fine Arts, Boston. All rights reserved. Gift of Miss Ellen A. Stone.*

ing attire. Mr. Robbins's death occurred during the most productive years of the lace industry, and the black lace lent itself nicely to the embellishment of funeral attire. Whether Mrs. Robbins wore this cape to her husband's funeral remains unknown, but it can be said that the cape was made around the time of his death. Widow Robbins died on January 3, 1802, at the age of sixty-three. Her cape became part of the wardrobe of daughter, Caira Robbins, 1794–1881.[6] It stayed in the family and was donated to the Museum of Fine Arts in Boston on October 15, 1899, by Miss Ellen A. Stone. Miss Stone was related to the Whipples of Ipswich and to the Robbins family.

Mrs. Robbins's cape is a beautiful example of how Ipswich lace was worn. It is interesting to note that the cape was not made by the same person who made the lace—the lace is sewn onto the garment with the wrong side facing out. This detail is something only a lace maker would see after close study.

Further study of the cape led to several notable discoveries. This cape contains two styles of the black Ipswich lace. One of them is identical to samples of lace at the Library of Congress. Compare the detail of the lace from the cape in fig. 77 to fig. 52, the sample at the Library of Congress. The pasteboard pricking from which both of these pieces was made can still be found at the Whipple House in Ipswich. The lace on this cape and hood is clearly Ipswich lace.

*Edward Henry Little*

The garment in fig. 78 provided many surprises, the first being that it was worn exclusively by males. The second discovery was that it has lace of the type made in Ipswich but in a blonde silk instead of the familiar black silk.

*Fig. 78.* Boy's dress with lace of the type made in Ipswich. Silk and linen, maker unknown. ca. 1795–1798. Displayed at the Cushing House Museum, in 1985, its exhibition label records that the dress was originally made for and worn by Eleazer Johnson. *Courtesy of the Historical Society of Old Newbury, gift of Eleanor Little Baker.*

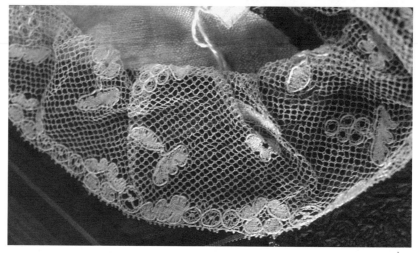

*Fig. 79.* Detail of lace on boy's dress, showing it to be the type made in Ipswich. Blonde silk, ca. 1795–1798. Displayed at the Cushing House Museum, in 1985. *Courtesy of the Historical Society of Old Newbury, gift of Eleanor Little Baker.*

The dress has a remarkable history attached to it. It was made between 1795 and 1798 and worn by Eleazer Johnson (1790–1870), a twin son of Captain William Pierce Johnson. Wearing this dress became a tradition for the young males of the family. The dress was passed down to Eleazer Johnson Jr., who continued the tradition. Fig. 80 shows Edward Henry Little (1879–1919), who was the grandson of Eleazer Johnson Jr., wearing the dress when he was around eight years of age. He later had his own children's portraits made wearing the dress.[7]

The dress is in remarkably good condition considering that it is made of silk. The bright colors of the dress—vermilion, ocher, black, and gold—are striking. The lace is of the type made in Ipswich. Close examination shows design elements, thread, and technical details consistent with Ipswich lace. (See fig. 79.) During the construction of this garment the Ipswich lace industry was in high production. Newburyport was one of the markets to which the lace was routinely taken to trade for goods. Many Ipswich families moved between Ipswich and Newburyport. One of Ipswich's most noted lace makers and lace merchants was Mary Boardman, who married Thomas Caldwell of Newburyport two months after her twentieth birthday. It is not surprising that Ipswich lace found its way into Newburyport to be used in the making of the Johnson/Little dress, but silk lace is always a rare find.

*Fig. 80.* Edward Henry Little (1879–1919) wearing the boy's dress as it was passed down to him. Photograph from 1887. *Courtesy of the Historical Society of Old Newbury, gift of Eleanor Little Baker.*

The Johnson/Little collection arrived at the Historical Society of Old Newbury in a lovely old trunk. A woman's cape also was found in the trunk (see fig. 81). It too is adorned with a blonde silk lace consistent in technique, materials, and design with the laces made in Ipswich (see fig. 82). It was made at about the same time as the boy's dress and is preserved for future study at the Historical Society of Old Newbury.

Many examples of Ipswich lace are packed away, quietly waiting to tell the tale of this remarkable American industry and of the people who worked in it. To some the lack of perfection in Ipswich lace is a disappointment. However, in the context of real history it is to be admired. The regal laces that often capture attention were made in regions of the world where lace making had been established for generations. Professional lace makers were trained in the notable schools of their area. Ipswich women faced a much different reality. They were transported to a new country and separated from the resources of home. There were no lace schools in America to teach refined techniques. The women learned from each other as time and opportunity allowed. Through the fabric and dynamics of their community they forged a small industry that spoke clearly of the realities of their day—the value of home and community

*Fig. 81.* Woman's cape, silk with silk lace, ca. 1795–1798. *Courtesy of the Historical Society of Old Newbury, gift of Eleanor Little Baker.*

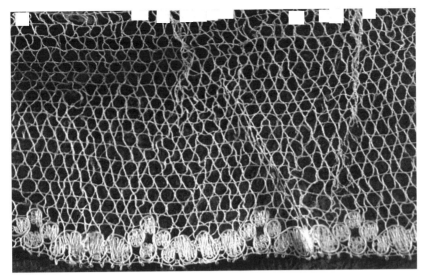

*Fig. 82.* Detail of lace on a woman's cape. Lace is of the type made in Ipswich. Blonde silk lace, ca. 1795–1798. *Courtesy of the Historical Society of Old Newbury, gift of Eleanor Little Baker.*

in the face of war and separation and the will to endure. These women produced lace under the most difficult circumstances and made it available to the average American. The dignity of wearing lace, whether for pleasure or patriotism, symbolizes the spirit of the people who envisioned a land of freedom and fought for its beginning.

Had fate allowed the skills of the women of Ipswich to evolve, it is likely that they too would have established a lace school, and over time the techniques would have been refined. But changes in fashion and the inventions of industry closed off that opportunity. What they did have the opportunity to do was to contribute to the history of a new nation that valued hard work and ingenuity.

5. A MATTER OF CLASS AND PRIDE

1. For more information on the work of William Jennys, see William Bright Jones, "The Portraits of Richard and William Jennys and the Story of Their Wayfaring Lives," in the *Dublin Seminar for Early New England Folklife, Annual Proceedings* (1994), vol. 19, *Painting and Portrait Making in the American Northeast* (Boston: Boston University Press, 1996), p. 64.

2. *The Papers of George Washington*, ed. W. W. Abbot and Dorothy Twohig, Presidential Series no. 4, September 1789–January 1790 (Charlottesville: University Press of Virginia, 1993), pp. 485–86.

3. Ibid., p. 218.

4. Joseph B. Felt, *History of Ipswich, Essex, and Hamilton* (Cambridge, Mass.: 1834; reprint, Ipswich, Mass.: Clamshell Press, 1966), p. 206.

5. Thomas Franklin Waters, *Ipswich in The Massachusetts Bay Colony*; Vol. 2, *A History of the Town from 1700–1917* (Ipswich, Mass.: Ipswich Historical Society, 1917), p. 369.

6. Ellen A. Stone, "Diary and Letters of Caira Robbins," *Lexington Historical Society Proceedings* 4 (1905–1910): 61–81.

7. Peter Benes, *Old-Town and the Waterside, Two Hundred Years of Tradition and Change in Newbury, Newburyport, and West Newbury, 1635–1835* (Newburyport, Mass.: Historical Society of Old Newbury, 1986), p. 173.

# ∞ EPILOGUE

*To Never Be Forgotten*

---

WITH THE FOUNDING of the Ipswich Historical Society, Miss Charlotte Jones, Mrs. Carrie B. Ladd (see fig. 83), and others in Ipswich participated in a revival of lace making from the early 1900s through the 1940s. Even though lace making was revived as a hobby, not a commercial enterprise, these women were proud of their lace-making heritage and well aware of the type of laces made in Ipswich. This is evident in an amusing story of a lace teacher from the Boston Museum School who was invited to teach lace making at the Whipple House in Ipswich. She was very quickly dismissed by the ladies because she made lace of "the wrong sort." She made the grievous mistake of trying to teach them Honiton lace.

The Colonial Revival certainly played a role in restoring an interest in preserving the things of the past. Thomas Frank Waters did his part by recording the history of Ipswich, as did Joseph Felt before him. Sarah E. Lakeman, a descendant of one of the lace-making families of Ipswich, was the spokesperson for Ipswich lace during her lifetime. She taught lace making, recounted the oral traditions regarding the lace industry, and gave lectures on lace, especially her beloved Ipswich lace. Miss Lakeman's lace collection can be found at the Ipswich Historical Society and at the Society for the Preservation of New England Antiquities.

A contemporary of hers was Mabel Foster Bainbridge, who also taught lace making and collected lace. Her collection can be found at the Valentine Museum in Richmond, Virginia. Mabel Bainbridge wrote an interesting article on Ipswich Lace for *House and Garden*, April 1916. Titled "Early Lace-Making in America," it is one of the better early articles, based on what was known at that time.

After the years of Carrie B. Ladd, Sarah E. Lakeman, and Mabel Bainbridge, Elizabeth Newton became the curator of the Whipple House. Her tireless efforts to preserve the lace collection at Ipswich are still remembered. With lace making alive and well in New England and throughout

*Fig. 83.* Miss Carrie B. Ladd in costume making lace at the Whipple House in Ipswich.
*Courtesy, Ipswich Historical Society, Ipswich, Massachusetts.*

the United States and Europe, lace making will not be forgotten in Ipswich, nor will the industry for which the town is known.

This research has been a journey of discovery into the lives of early Americans. Primary research is not easy, but the headstone of the grave of Elizabeth Foster Sutton, to whom this text is dedicated, was a constant encouragement. Elizabeth died on October 29, 1805. On a bitter cold day when I first wiped away snow from her gravestone I was struck by the words "My friends and children, when this you see, remember me."

I wondered when someone had last visited her grave. I hope that in some modest way this research will shed light on the details of a remarkable American industry and that more research will be done in the future, not only on Ipswich lace but on the richness of American textiles. May Elizabeth get her last wish, and may the work of so many hands not be forgotten.

# Appendixes

## THE LETTERS OF JOSEPH DANA

These letters contain some of the most thoroughly documented information on the industry of lace making at Ipswich. The handwritten text is transcribed here for the convenience of the reader. Copies of these letters also may be found in *Industrial and Commercial Correspondence of Alexander Hamilton, Anticipating His Report on Manufactures*, edited by Arthur Harrison Cole (New York: Augustus M. Kelley Publishers, 1968).

*To The Honorable George Cabot Esq of Beverly*
*From Joseph Dana*
*July 26, 1790*

*Sir,*

At first receiving your fav of June 17th I indulged the hope of transmitting in short time the desired intelligence from this town; and therefore did not write immediately; as it seemed more agreeable to make answer by doings than by promises.

But as the business will require more time than was at first apprehended; this line, Sir, will acquaint you that I am attending to it, as my moments of leisure will allow; and endeavouring to engage as many others in it, as will be accurate in the parts which they undertake. And this is done the more cheerfully, as well as from the source where it originates, we have full confidence, that the ultimate object is to befriend the manufacturers of our country, and not to take advantage of them.

There are indeed (unless we number the common mechanical arts, which, I conceive, is not the intention) There are, within my knowledge, not more than two kinds of manufacture in this town. The one is of Cordage (in the parish of Chebacco), of which I hope to receive a seasonable return. The other is of lace; the machinery, indeed very simple—consisting only of a round or perhaps elliptical pillow, from 8 to 12 inches diameter; a strip of parchment or pasteboard, encircling the same, (upon which the pattern of the lace is pricked out) a few rows of pins; and bobbins—from a dozen to 120, according to the width & figure of the pattern. But the work itself is in a dispersed Situation; there being in the different parts of this town, probably not less than 600 persons who do more or less in it; some devoting the most of their time to; other, little intervals only: some employed in the smaller patterns, others in the larger and more complex; and all independent of each other—So that to ascertain "the quantity and value of the annual finished work," is an undertaking of some difficulty.

We are willing never the less, to be at some pains for the purpose; as it is probable that this manufacture would be most worthy of some attention, if its magnitude were known with the height to which it is carried in many instances and the perfection to which the whole might arrive, by a little encouragemt.

As early, Sir, as circumstances will admit, You will receive the result of our enquiries. In the mean time I subscribe, with every sentiment of esteem & veneration,

 *Sir,*

  *Your very obedient*
   *and humble Servant*
    *Joseph Dana*


*To The Honorable George Cabot Esq of Beverly*
*From Joseph Dana*
*January 24, 1791*

*Sir,*

The inclosed return of the Ipswich Lace manufacture, has been ready more than three months, and only waiting to be accompanied by the Acct of looms, weaving &c. which, altho made out in part, is not yet compleated throughout the town. The acct now transmitted, I believe to be a candid one; and as exact as recollection could make it; Most of the families were waited upon twice, by the young ladies who undertook this enquiry.

You will receive, Sir, with this, some specimens of the work; And if returns are to be made to the Secretary of the Treasury by way of the Academy [American Academy of Arts and Sciences], it is asked as an indulgence, that these specimens, after being inspected by that honorable Body, may pass on, under their direction, so as to be ultimately presented to the beloved President of the United States, and to his Consort.

If things fall out otherwise, And returns are not to be made thro' the Academy, within a short time; it is requested, Sir, that in that case, the patterns may remain in your hands; And that your friendship to the manufacturers of our country, may induce you to accept the obliging office of presenting them, as before mentioned, when you shall go to the Seat of the Federal government.

On the latter supposition, there may be opp for some of us to wait on you with our wishes upon this subject; As I should have done at this time, had not special engagements put it out of my power. I am, Sir, with the highest respect,

  *Your very obedient*
   *and humble Servant,*
    *Joseph Dana*

## SOURCES FOR MODERN DAY LACE MAKERS

The following is a listing of some of the resources available to those interested in learning to make lace.

To find lace teachers and more information about lace making and supplies contact International Old Lacers, P.O. Box 554, Flanders, NJ 07836.

This organization can give you lists of teachers and suppliers in your area, and they publish a bulletin that covers current events and lace-making issues. They also have a wonderful library of books and lace-making videos. It is very worthwhile to become involved in the group. Local guilds of lace makers are available in nearly every area of the United States, and they meet on a regular basis to make lace, learn new techniques, and share the fun of lace making.

While I am certain that there are large numbers of excellent suppliers and teachers, I recommend Holly Van Sciver and Robin's Bobbins because I know them and I am familiar with the high quality of their work and supplies. Both Holly and Robin are outstanding lace instructors and very knowledgeable. Either one can provide information on suppliers and teachers outside the United States.

Robin's Bobbins
1674 Murphy Hwy.
Mineral Bluff, GA 30559–9736

VanSciver Bobbin Lace
130 Cascadilla Park
Ithaca, NY 14850

*Other Resources*

Arbor House, 22 Arbor Lane, Roslyn Heights, NY 11577
Beggars' Lace, P.O. Box 481223, Denver, CO 80248
Berga Ullman Inc., P.O. Box 918, North Adams, MA 01247
Bobbins by Van-Dieren, 2304 Clifford Avenue, Rochester, NY 14609–3825
Debbie A comfi-Shuttle, 13716 NE 50th Avenue, Vancouver, WA 98686
Frederick J. Fawcett, 129 South Street, Boston, MA 02130
Grandmother's Lace Remembered, 1652 LaMar Dr., North Mankato,
    MN 56003

Happy Hands, 3007 S. W. Marshall, Pendleton, OR 97180

Hensel Productions, P.O. Box 825, Marcola, OR 97454

*International Lace Magazine*, editorial office, Lieve A. Jerger-Baekelmans, 1621 West 25th Street, San Pedro, CA 90732

Kathy Kirchner, 790 University Place, Grosse Pointe City, MI 48230–1263

The Lacemaker, 23732-G Bothell Hwy, SE, Bothell, WA 98021

The Lace Merchant, P.O. Box 222, Plainwell, MI 49080

Lace Place de Begique, 800 S.W. 17th Street, Boca Raton, FL 33432

Lacis, 3163 Adeline Street, Berkeley, CA 94703

Robin and Russ Handweavers, 533 North Adams Street, McMinnville, OR 97128

Some Place, 2990 Adeline Street, Berkeley, CA 94703

Osma G. Todd Studio, 319 Mednoza Avenue, Coral Gables, FL 33134

Woodturnings (lace bobbins), 642 Pine Ridge St., Perry, GA 31069

The World in Stitches, 82 South Street, Milford, NH 03055

## PATTERNS FOR MAKING IPSWICH LACE

This section provides prickings and working diagrams for making Ipswich lace. The laces represented in this section could be considered classic Ipswich laces in that the patterns are well documented and were part of the actual patterns used in the Ipswich lace industry.

Some very good lace makers prefer to work from the original prickings, complete with their inconsistent grids and less than straight edges. Their rightful concern is that in making any change in the original pattern something inherently a part of the lace could be lost. And their concerns are certainly justified. Other very good lace makers feel that "trued" patterns with straight edges and even grids can reflect the intentions of the original. I have a great appreciation for both concepts and the concerns of each. A study of Ipswich laces has shown, in my opinion, that lines that wandered a little were intended to be straight, and the grids became less than uniform only out of hurried production and overuse of prickings. Therefore, the following prickings are offered for the benefit of modern lace makers.

These prickings are from the original prickings and lace samples. They have been altered in only two ways: the grid of the groundwork areas has been made consistent, and the straight lines have been made straight.

These patterns include a photograph of the reproduced lace, reference to the illustration of the original lace whenever possible, a pricking, and a working diagram. Some general instructions are provided. Detailed instructions were not possible due to the constraints of publishing; however, the experienced lace maker will find that the stitches are familiar ones. It is suggested that these diagrams be photocopied and color-coded in the standard method. For more information on stitches and color coding, see Robin Lewis-Wild, *101 Torchon Patterns with Coloured Technical Diagrams* (London: B. T. Batsford, 1993), p. viii. The author uses the same visual method of documenting patterns.

The thread for the following patterns depends greatly on the preferences of the lace maker and the size of the pricking. I do suggest that starting with white thread is easiest. Once the lace maker is familiar with the pattern, switching to the black silk produces a lovely soft lace.

*Pricking No. 1*

This lace was reproduced by Sheryl DeJong. It can be seen on the portrait of Mrs. Hezekiah Beardsley (fig. 73). A sample of this lace is at the Library of Congress (see fig. 61).

Thread is black silk. Footside is worked on the left. Sheryl used 22 pairs and gimps, added a gimp at each diamond, and used 3 pairs inside the oval shapes at the header. The groundwork is the Brussels/Mechlin type (CTCT.CTCT) followed by 1 or 2 twists between stitches. The diamonds are worked in a cloth stitch, as are the motifs on the header. Picots are done with seven twists total.

*Fig. 84.* Reproduction of Ipswich lace by Sheryl DeJong in black silk, 45 mm. *Used with permission, courtesy of Sheryl DeJong.*

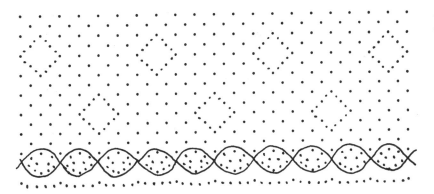

*Fig. 85.* Pricking. *Courtesy of Sheryl DeJong.*

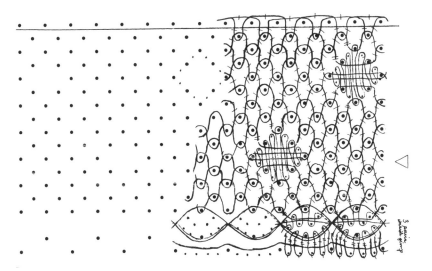

*Fig. 86.* Working Diagram. *Courtesy of Sheryl DeJong.*

*Pricking No. 2*

This lace is one of the most commonly seen of the Ipswich white laces (see fig. 10). Samples can be found on many children's garments throughout New England and in several variations on many Ipswich pillows (see fig. 12), such as Mrs. Low's pillow (fig. 10). The Whipple House in Ipswich has dozens of prickings with this pattern or variations of it.

In the beginning of this research the prickings were a bit puzzling, as the prickings from this era don't have any markings to guide the lace maker. At first glance the prickings looked like four simple rows of pinholes. Study soon matched the prickings with their laces. The pattern included here is approximately 20 mm in depth; the original lace in this pattern ranged from 10 to 15 mm. To make the narrower laces this pattern can be reduced with the use of a good copy machine.

This lace is fun to make. The thread is either linen or cotton. The footside is on the left. Seven pairs plus a gimp pair are used.

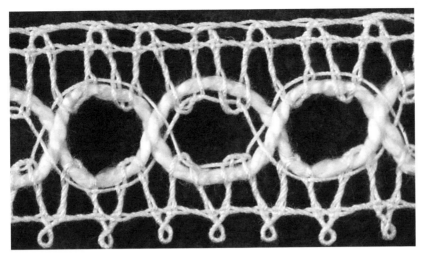

*Fig. 87.* Reproduction of Ipswich lace by Agnes V. Breemen in white cotton or linen, 20 mm. *Used with permission, courtesy of Agnes V. Breemen.*

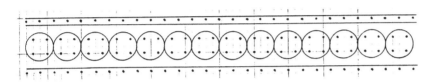

*Fig. 88.* Pricking. *Courtesy of Agnes V. Breemen.*

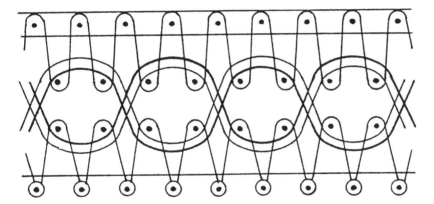

*Fig. 89.* Working Diagram. *Courtesy of Agnes V. Breemen.*

## Pricking No. 3

This lace is from one of the samples at the Library of Congress (see figs. 62 and 63), and the pricking for the piece is at the Whipple House in Ipswich (see fig. 21). In oral tradition this particular pattern is proudly recalled as one of the patterns original to Ipswich. As this research has shown, oral traditions can be mistaken; however, this is certainly one of the more interesting of the Ipswich patterns.

The thread is black silk. The footside is worked on the left. The groundwork is the Torchon type with an extra twist at the pin (CTT.CTT). It is the same thing as a honeycomb but worked on a regular grid. The main fill is a half stitch outlined in gimp. The unusual fill in these motifs is a series of spiders.

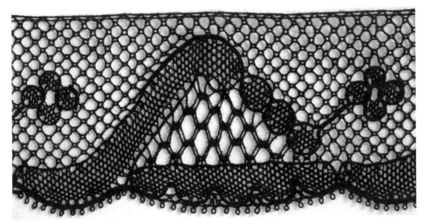

*Fig. 90.* Reproduction of Ipswich lace by Agnes V. Breemen in black silk, 50 mm. *Used with permission, courtesy of Agnes V. Breemen.*

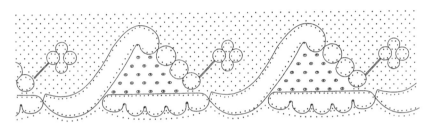

*Fig. 91.* Pricking. *Courtesy of Agnes V. Breemen.*

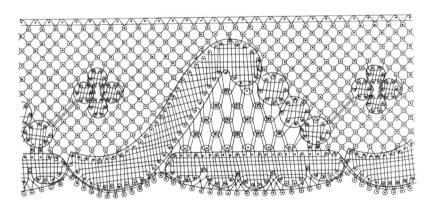

*Fig. 92.* Working Diagram. *Courtesy of Agnes V. Breemen.*

*Pricking No. 4*

This lace is from one of the samples at the Whipple House (see fig. 38). It was made of black silk and is the only sample of the original black laces within the collection at Ipswich. Most of the black laces have survived with the letters of Joseph Dana at the Library of Congress, George Washington's Mt. Vernon, and the Museum of Fine Arts, Boston.

The thread is black silk. The footside is worked on the left. Forty-one pairs are used, plus gimp. The fills include half stitch, point ground (as you know from Bucks ground or Chantilly ground), open peas, and an Old Mayflower fill. The groundwork is a kat stitch or Paris ground. I would recommend this pattern for those with a fair amount of experience or a great sense of adventure.

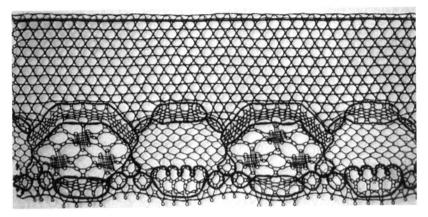

*Fig. 93.* Reproduction of Ipswich lace by Christa Van Schagen in black silk, 47 mm. *Used with permission, courtesy of Christa Van Schagen.*

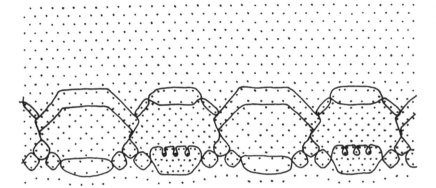

*Fig. 94.* Pricking. *Courtesy of Christa Van Schagen.*

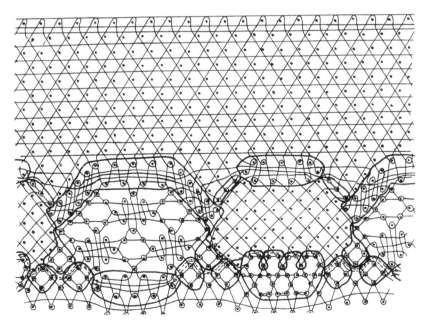

*Fig. 95.* Working Diagram. *Courtesy of Christa Van Schagen.*

*Pricking No. 5*

This lace is from one of the samples at the Library of Congress (see fig. 29). The pattern is interesting in that it reflects the influence of the heavy metal laces used on early furnishings.

The thread is black silk. The footside is worked on the left. Fifty pairs are used, plus gimp. The groundwork is the kat stitch or Paris ground. The fills are half stitch, single spider, open peas, and the Torchon-type ground with the extra twist at the pinhole, combined with small tally-like squares worked in a cloth stitch.

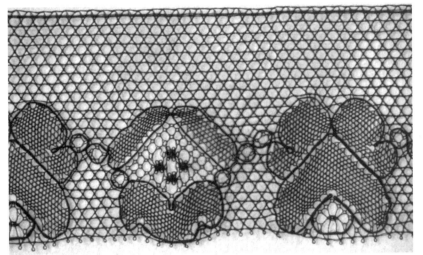

*Fig. 96.* Reproduction of Ipswich lace by Christa Van Schagen in black silk, 58 mm. *Used with permission, courtesy of Christa Van Schagen.*

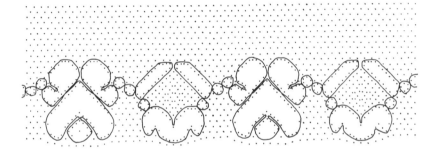

*Fig. 97.* Pricking. *Courtesy of Christa Van Schagen.*

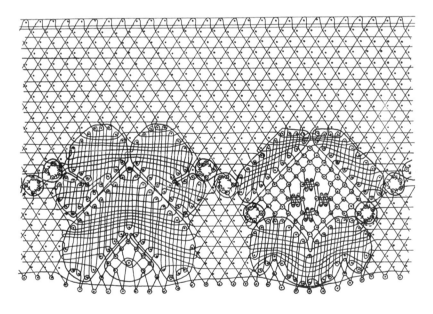

*Fig. 98.* Working Diagram. *Courtesy of Christa Van Schagen.*

*Pricking No. 6*

This lace is from one of the samples at the Library of Congress (see fig. 52); the pricking for the piece is at the Whipple House in Ipswich on the lace pillow of Lydia Lord Lakeman. The lace can be found on a woman's cape at the Museum of Fine Arts, Boston (see fig. 77).

After I worked my way through the header of this piece, this pattern became one of my personal favorites. The thread is black silk. The footside is worked on the left. The groundwork is the Torchon type with an extra twist at the pinhole. The fills are cloth stitch. The picots are worked with a total of seven twists. The motifs on the header may be worked with gimp or with regular thread.

It is my hope that you enjoy exploring these lace patterns. They have deliberately been presented without volumes of detailed instructions. They are terrific exercises in problem solving and advancing the understanding of the dynamics of lace. Just as each musician interprets Bach with subtle differences, I have no doubt that each lace maker will interpret the lace in slightly different ways. And why not? This was also true of the Ipswich lace makers. Each had her own way of working the footing or making a picot or attaching the gimp. Explore, delve, study, scrutinize, observe, ponder, search, investigate . . . above all learn and enjoy this wonderful art of lace making.

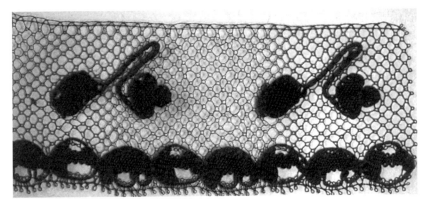

*Fig. 99.* Reproduction of Ipswich lace by Lia Baumeister in black silk, 44 mm. *Used with permission, courtesy of Lia Baumeister.*

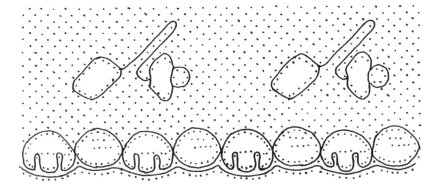

*Fig. 100.* Pricking. *Courtesy of Lia Baumeister.*

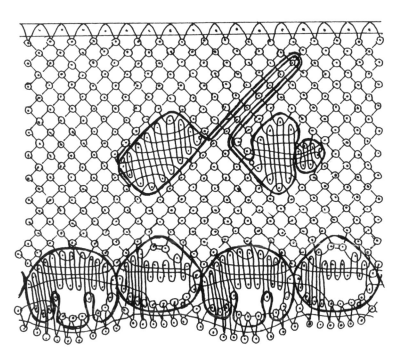

*Fig. 101.* Working Diagram. *Courtesy of Lia Baumeister.*

# Glossary of Lace-Making Terms

This brief glossary is intended as a quick reference for the convenience of readers, especially those new to the technical aspects of lace and lace making. There are many more types of lace and lace-making terms not included in this brief listing. For further reading on this subject, see the bibliography.

Bayeux:  A continuous bobbin lace made in France that resembles Chantilly.

Blonde:  A straight or continuous bobbin lace originally made in France of silk thread in the eighteenth and nineteenth centuries. Originally, this lace was made with silk in its natural, or blonde, color; later specimens were made in black-dyed silk.

Bobbins:  A method for holding the thread neatly in place that allows the lace maker to manipulate the threads without touching them directly. The weight of the bobbin puts tension on the threads during the production of the lace. Bobbins have been made in many materials, most commonly woods, reeds, bone, and glass.

Bobbin lace, bone lace, thread lace, or pillow lace:  A handmade lace produced with bobbins and a technique that is similar to weaving. "Thread lace" is a common eighteenth-century term for handmade bobbin lace made from linen thread.

Bucks Point, Buckingham, Buckinghamshire:  An English bobbin lace made from the sixteenth century to the twenty-first century that reached its full development in the nineteenth century. This continuous type of bobbin lace resembles the French Lille and is sometimes referred to as English Lille. The designs can be either geometric or floral. The groundwork is measured at 52–60 degrees.

Chantilly:  A continuous type of bobbin lace that dates from the seventeenth century to the twenty-first century and originated in France. It was usually made in silk. Chantilly lace made with black silk became very popular. This lace was produced in narrow strips that were then joined with a ingenious stitch that left no detectable seam. The most striking feature of Chantilly, beyond its abundant detail, is the remarkable effect of light and shadow created by the use of a half stitch and whole stitch as a fill during the nineteenth century.

Crochet: In its simplest form, a type of lace made from one strand of yarn and worked into a pattern with a crochet hook. There are many different types of crochet, each distinct from the other, such as Irish crochet, broomstick crochet, and filet.

Dressed pillow: A completely assembled lace pillow with pricking, bobbins with thread, pins, lace pocket, and pincushion ready for making lace.

Fill, Fillings: Decorative lace-making stitches used to fill in a space within the design elements of a piece of lace. For example, the shape of a leaf could be filled in with a cloth stitch, a half stitch, or a combination of both.

Flax, Linen: The natural fibers that come from the flax plant, *Linum usitatissimum*. The long fibers of flax are spun into thread that is suitable for making lace.

Foot, Footside: The straight or sewing edge of lace usually attached or sewn to a garment.

Gimp: A thread applied to outline a decorative element in bobbin lace. The gimp thread is usually heavier than the threads used in the rest of the lace, which gives definition to the design.

Hairpin lace: A type of airy lace made by using a device that resembles a large hairpin. This lace is frequently classified as a type of crochet.

Honiton: An English lace of the noncontinuous type made from the sixteenth century to the twenty-first century.

Knitted lace: A lace made by using fine yarn, fine knitting needles, and the techniques of knitting.

Parchment: (1) A pricking made from sheepskin, or (2) an animal hide or skin treated in such a way that it can be used to write on. The remarkable durability of parchment makes it an excellent material for prickings.

Passives: The threads in bobbin lace making that hang straight or passively while other threads or pairs of bobbins work through these threads in a weaving manner to create the lace stitches.

Picot: A small decorative stitch resembling a tiny loop used on the header edge of bobbin lace.

Pillow: A firm foundation on which lace is made.

Point de Paris: A type of groundwork found in bobbin laces that resembles a six-point star. This type of ground can be found in French and English laces and is also known as kat stitch or wire ground. There is also a lace called Point de Paris that was made in France from the seventeenth century that employed the Point de Paris ground.

Pricker: A small sharp instrument used to create a pattern of pinholes in a parchment for making a pricking.

Pricking: A template-like pattern on which bobbin lace is made. Each pricking has a pattern of holes "pricked out," which allows for the placement of pins as the lace is worked.

Silk: A natural protein filament from the cocoons of silkworms that can be used to make thread appropriate for lace making.

Spangles: Small beads attached to the bottom of a bobbin. These spangles are both decorative and functional. They give weight to the bobbin, which holds tension on the threads as the lace is worked, and they prevent the bobbin from rolling.

Tatting: A type of knotted lace made with one or two threads and a small shuttle.

Thread count or weight: A relative measure of the fineness of a thread used in making lace. According to Pat Earnshaw, "A count is the number of skeins of flax, each 300 yards long, required to make up a pound weight."

Torchon: A type of continuous bobbin lace most often, but not always, made in geometric designs. It may be considered a universal lace as it is one of the simplest and oldest laces and is common to many lace-making regions. Torchon lace is often the first lace a new lace maker learns before moving on to the more complex laces.

# Bibliography

"American Speech: 1600 to the Present." *Dublin Seminar for New England Folklife, Annual Proceedings 1983.* (1985).

Bainbridge, Mabel Foster. "Early Lace-Making in America," *House and Garden,* April 1916.

Benes, Peter. *Old-Town and the Waterside: Two Hundred Years of Tradition and Change in Newbury, Newburyport, and West Newbury, 1635–1835.* Catalog of an exhibition at the Cushing House Museum, Newburyport, Massachusetts. Newburyport, Mass: Historical Society of Old Newbury, 1986.

Bishop, John Leander. *A History of American Manufactures from 1608 to 1860.* London: Edward Young & Co., 1868.

Bober, Natalie S. *Abigail Adams: Witness to a Revolution.* New York: Aladdin Paperbacks, 1998.

Cole, Arthur Harrison, ed. *Industrial and Commercial Correspondence of Alexander Hamilton, Anticipating His Report on Manufactures,* New York: Augustus M. Kelley, 1968.

Cooke, Jacob Ernest. *Tench Coxe and the Early Republic.* Chapel Hill: University of North Carolina Press, for the Institute of Early American History and Culture, Williamsburg, Va., 1978.

Earnshaw, Pat. *A Dictionary of Lace.* Princes Risborough, Buckinghamshire, UK: Shire Publications, 1982.

———. *The Identification of Lace.* Princes Risborough, Buckinghamshire, UK: Shire Publications, 1994.

———. *Threads of Lace, from Source to Sink.* Guildford, UK: Gorse Publications, 1989.

Emery, Irene. *Primary Structures of Fabrics: An Illustrated Classification.* New York: Thames and Hudson, 1994.

Felt, Joseph B. *History of Ipswich, Essex, and Hamilton.* Cambridge, Mass., 1834. Reprint, Ipswich, Mass.: Clamshell Press, 1966.

Fewkes, Jesse. "Fine Thread, Lace, and Hosiery." In *Proceedings of the Annual Meeting, Ipswich Historical Society.* Salem, Mass.: Salem Press, 1904.

Ginsburg, Madeleine, ed. *The Illustrated History of Textiles,* London: Studio Editions, 1991, 1995.

Gwynne, Judyth L. *The Illustrated Dictionary of Lace.* Berkeley, Calif.: Lacis Publications, 1997.

Hammatt, Abraham. *The Hammatt Papers: Early Inhabitants of Ipswich, Massachusetts, 1633–1700*. Baltimore: Genealogy Publishing Co., 1980.

"House and Home." *Dublin Seminar for New England Folklife, Annual Proceedings 1988*. (1990).

Johnson, Arthur W., and Ralph E. Ladd Jr. *Memento Mori*. Ipswich Mass.: Ipswich Historical Society, 1935.

Kurella, Elizabeth M. *The Secrets of Real Lace*. Plainwell, Mich: Lace Merchant, 1994.

Levey, Santina M. *Lace, A History*. London: Victoria and Albert Museum, 1983.

Morris, Frances. *Notes on Laces of the American Colonists*. New York: William Helburn, for Needle and Bobbin Club, 1926.

Morse, Jedidiah. *The American Gazetter, Exhibiting a Full Account of the Civil Divisions, Rivers, Harbours, Indian Tribes, etc. of the American Continent, also of the West India and other appendant Islands; with a Particular Description of Louisiana*. Boston: Samuel Etheridge, for Thomas and Andrews, 1797.

Nottingham, Pamela. *Bucks Point Lacemaking*. McMinnville, Oreg.: Robin & Russ Handweavers, 1985.

"Painting and Portrait Making in the American Northeast." *Dublin Seminar for New England Folklife, Annual Proceedings 1994*. (1995).

Palliser, Mrs. Bury. *History of Lace*. New York: Charles Scribner & Sons, 1911. Reprint, New York: Dover Publications, 1984.

Southard, Doris. *Lessons in Bobbin Lacemaking*. New York: Dover Publications, 1992.

Tapley, Harriet Silvester. *Chronicles of Danvers (Old Salem Village) Massachusetts, 1632–1923*, Danvers, Mass.: Danvers Historical Society, 1923.

"Textiles in Early New England: Design, Production, and Consumption." *Dublin Seminar for New England Folklife, Annual Proceedings 1997*. (1999).

Ulrich, Laurel Thatcher. *Goodwives: Image and Reality in the Lives of Women in Northern New England, 1650–1750*. New York: Vintage Books, 1991.

———. *A Midwife's Tale: The Life of Martha Ballard, Based on Her Diary, 1785–1812*. New York: Alfred A. Knopf, 1990; New York: Vintage Books, 1991.

Vanderpoel, Emily Noyes. *American Lace and Lace-Makers*. New Haven, Conn.: Yale University Press, 1924.

Vickers, Daniel. *Farmers and Fishermen: Two Centuries of Work in Essex County, Massachusetts, 1630–1850*. Chapel Hill: University of North Carolina Press, for the Institute of Early American History and Culture, Williamsburg, 1994.

Von Henneberg, Freiherr Alfred. *The Art and Craft of Old Lace*. by London: B. T. Batsford, 1931. Reprint, Berkeley, Calif.: Lacis Publications, 1999.

Waters, Thomas Franklin. *Ipswich in Massachusetts Bay Colony*. Vol. 1, *1633–1700*; Vol. 2, *1700–1917*. Ipswich, Mass.: Ipswich Historical Society, 1917.

———. "Ipswich Mills and Factories." In *Proceedings of the Annual Meeting, Ipswich Historical Society*. Salem, Mass.: Salem Press, 1904.

Weissman, Judith Reiter, and Wendy Lavitt. *Labors of Love: America's Textiles and Needlework, 1650–1930*. New York: Alfred A. Knopf, 1987.

LIBRARY OF CONGRESS CATALOGING-IN-PUBLICATION DATA

Raffel, Marta Cotterell
The laces of Ipswich : the art and economics of an early American
industry, 1750–1840 / Marta Cotterell Raffel
p.    cm.
Includes bibliographical references
ISBN 1–58465–163–6
1. Lace and lace making—Massachusetts—Ipswich.
2. Lace industry—Massachusetts—Ipswich.  I. Title.
NK9412.I67 C67 2003
746.2'2—dc21        2002015336